# GENESIS

*God*

## Makes a Start

*A Guided Discovery for Groups and Individuals*

**Kevin Perrotta**

LOYOLA PRESS.
A JESUIT MINISTRY

Chicago

# LOYOLA PRESS.
## A JESUIT MINISTRY

3441 N. Ashland Avenue
Chicago, Illinois 60657
(800) 621-1008
www.loyolapress.com

| | |
|---|---|
| *Imprimatur* | *Nihil Obstat* |
| Most Reverend Raymond E. Goedert, | Reverend Michael Mulhall, O.Carm. |
| M.A., S.T.L., J.C.L. | Censor Deputatus |
| Vicar General | February 29, 2000 |
| Archdiocese of Chicago | |
| February 29, 2000 | |

The *Nihil Obstat* and *Imprimatur* are official declarations that a book is free of doctrinal and moral error. No implication is contained therein that those who have granted the *Nihil Obstat* and *Imprimatur* agree with the content, opinions, or statements expressed.

The Scripture quotations contained herein are from the New Revised Standard Version Bible: Catholic Edition, copyright © 1993 and 1989 by the Division of Christian Education of the National Council of Churches of Christ in the U.S.A. Used by permission. All rights reserved. Subheadings in Scripture quotations have been added by Kevin Perrotta.

Bernadette McCarver Snyder's comment (p. 23) is from her book *Graham Crackers, Galoshes, and God: Everywoman's Book of Cope and Hope* (Liguori, Mo.: Liguori Publications, 1995).

The interview with Dom Helder Camara (p. 23) originally appeared in Oriana Fallaci, "Voice in the Wilderness," *The Sign,* July/August 1976.

Antoinette Bosco's comment (p. 23) is from her book *The Pummeled Heart: Finding Peace through Pain* (Mystic, Conn.: Twenty-Third Publications, 1994).

The Latin text of St. Augustine's commentary *De Genesi ad Litteram libri XII* (p. 35) can be found in J.-P. Migne, ed., *Patrologia Latina* (Paris, 1887), vols. 34–35: cols. 245–486. Translation by Kevin Perrotta.

The Syriac text of St. Ephrem the Syrian's *Hymns of Paradise* (p. 36) can be found in Edmund Beck, ed., *Des Heiligen Ephraem des Syrers Hymnen de Paradiso,* Corpus Scriptorum Christianorum Orientalium, vol. 174 (Louvain: Secreteriat du Corpus SCO, 1957). Translation by Kevin Perrotta.

The Greek text of St. John Chrysostom's homily on Genesis 17 (p. 47) can be found in J.-P. Migne, ed., *Patrologia Graeca* (Paris, 1862), vol. 53: cols. 134–48. Translation by Kevin Perrotta.

Jacques Fesch's reflections (p. 59) are from Augustin-Michel Lemonnier, ed., *Light over the Scaffold and Cell 18: The Prison Letters of Jacques Fesch* (New York: Alba House, 1996).

Jean Vanier's reminiscences (p. 71) are from his book *An Ark for the Poor* (New York: Crossroad Publishing, 1995). The prayer can be found in Kathryn Spink, *Jean Vanier and l'Arche: A Communion of Love* (New York: Crossroad Publishing, 1991).

*Interior design by Kay Hartmann/Communique Design*
*Illustration by Charise Mericle Harper*

ISBN-13: 978-0-8294-1445-5; ISBN-10: 0-8294-1445-2

Printed in the United States of America

08 09 10 11 12 13 14 Bang 10 9 8 7 6 5

# Contents

**4**   *How to Use This Guide*

**6**   *Exploring Our Beginnings*

**14**   **Week 1**
**Let There Be Light!**
Genesis 1:1–31

**26**   **Week 2**
**The First Marriage**
Genesis 2:4–25

**38**   **Week 3**
**Distrust, Disobedience, and Dismay**
Genesis 3:1–24

**50**   **Week 4**
**East of Eden**
Genesis 4:1–5:5

**62**   **Week 5**
**God Starts Over**
Genesis 6:5–9:11

**74**   **Week 6**
**The End of the Beginning**
Genesis 11:1–12:5

**86**   *A Book for Today*

**92**   *Suggestions for Bible Discussion Groups*

**95**   *Suggestions for Individuals*

**96**   *Resources*

## How to Use This Guide

The Bible is like a vast national park filled with various types of terrain and impressive natural features. The park is so big that you could spend months, even years, getting to know it. Is it worth making a brief visit?

In fact, a brief visit to a park, if carefully planned, can be enjoyable and worthwhile. In a few hours you can drive through the park and pull over at a handful of sites. At each stop you can get out of the car, take a short trail through the woods, listen to the wind blowing in the trees, get a feel for the place.

You might compare this booklet to a short visit to a national park. We will read sections of the first eleven chapters of Genesis, which contain the Bible's accounts of creation and the beginning of the human race. We will be able to take a leisurely walk through each account, thinking carefully about what we are reading and what it means for our lives today. While these chapters of Genesis are only a small fraction of the entire Bible, they touch on central themes in God's revelation to us: God's creative purposes for us, the effects of sin on our relationship with God, and God's continuing faithfulness toward us.

This guide provides everything you need to explore Genesis 1 through 11 in six discussions—or to do a six-part exploration on your own. The introduction (page 6) will prepare you to get the most out of your reading. The weekly sections provide explanations that highlight what the words of Scripture mean for us today. Equally important, each section supplies questions that will launch you into fruitful discussion, helping you both to explore Genesis for yourself and to learn from one another. If you're using the booklet by yourself, the questions will spur your personal reflection.

Each discussion is meant to be a *guided discovery*.

**Guided.** None of us is equipped to read the Bible without help. We read the Bible *for* ourselves but not *by* ourselves. Scripture was written to be understood and applied in and with the Church. So each week "A Guide to the Reading," drawing on the work of modern biblical scholars and Christian writers of the past, supplies background and explanations. The guide will help you grasp the messages of Genesis. Think of it as a friendly park ranger who points out noteworthy details and explains what you're looking at so you can appreciate things for yourself.

**Discovery.** The purpose is for *you* to interact with God's Word. "Questions for Careful Reading" is a tool to help you dig into the Genesis accounts and examine them carefully. "Questions for Application" will help you consider what these stories mean for your life here and now. Each week concludes with an "Approach to Prayer" section that helps you respond to God's Word. Supplementary "Living Tradition" and "Saints in the Making" sections offer the thoughts and experiences of Christians past and present in order to show you what Scripture has meant to others—so that you can consider what it might mean for you.

**How long are the discussion sessions?** We've assumed you will have about an hour and a half when you get together. If you have less time, you'll find that most of the elements can be shortened somewhat.

**Is homework necessary?** You will get the most out of the discussions if you read the weekly material in advance of each meeting. But if participants are not able to prepare, have someone read the "What's Happened" and "Guide to the Reading" sections aloud to the group at the points where they occur in the weekly material.

**What about leadership?** If you happen to have a world-class biblical scholar in your group, by all means ask him or her to lead the discussions. But in the absence of any professional Scripture scholars, or even accomplished biblical amateurs, you can still have a first-class Bible discussion. Choose two or three people to be facilitators, and have everyone read "Suggestions for Bible Discussion Groups" before beginning (page 92).

**Does everyone need a guide? a Bible?** Everyone in the group will need their own copy of this booklet. It contains the text of the portions of Genesis that you will be reading, so a Bible is not absolutely necessary—but each participant will find it useful to have one. You should have at least one Bible on hand for your discussion. (See page 96 for recommendations.)

**How do we get started?** Before you begin, take a look at the suggestions for Bible discussion groups (page 92) and individuals (page 95).

I n the beginning . . ." The absolute beginning—*the* beginning—
fascinates us. The astrophysicist is not the only person drawn
to ponder the big bang, that first moment when a mysterious
little gift package of particles and forces arrived from nowhere,
unwrapped itself, and exploded into a universe of galaxies, planets,
mountain ranges, oak trees, and robins. The beginning is a magnet
for all of us because it is *our* beginning.

So it is natural for us to be intrigued by Genesis. Genesis
is the book famous for beginning, "In the beginning." Not only the
first chapter but also the next ten chapters recount the origins of
the universe and humankind. These are God-inspired accounts of
our beginnings. Of course we are interested.

When we open the Bible to the first page, however, we find
things strange by modern standards. Genesis is unlike modern
books on cosmic or human origins. Here is no astronomer's account
of a big bang and an expanding universe, no biologist's sketch of
life evolving over a billion years. In Genesis 1 the interval from dark
emptiness to human beings is spanned in six days. There is no
paleontologist's report on early toolmaking hominids, but vivid,
tragic tales of creation, harmony, sin, and judgment.

Familiarity may have dulled our surprise at the strangeness
of Genesis. Pretty much everyone has heard of Adam and Eve and
Cain and Noah. But as we set out to learn more from these stories,
a good starting point is a fresh sense of how unusual they are.

The early chapters of Genesis remind me of a contest con-
ducted from time to time in a magazine called *Biblical Archaeology
Review.* The editors publish a photograph of an artifact excavated
somewhere in the Near East and challenge readers to identify it.
A picture of one three-thousand-year-old item was accompanied
by these questions: "What is it? A ceremonial axe head? an ivory
earring? handcuffs? game board? pasta maker?" Looking at the
picture, you could believe it was any or none of those things (it
turned out to be a board for playing a long-forgotten game called
Fifty-eight Holes). The editors choose ancient items that are different from anything made or used today—which is the point of
similarity to Genesis. The types of writing we meet in Genesis

chapters 1–11 are also different from those we are familiar with today.

The main reason for this difference is that the authors of Genesis, like the people who played Fifty-eight Holes, belonged to a world quite unlike our own. They lived before the rise of scientific thinking. They did not have modern methods of writing history. They did much of their theologizing through stories. This is not to say they were primitive or unintelligent. They were as capable of wisdom as any later people, and God guided them in a unique way to compose the work that he intended. Nevertheless, the book they produced is the product of *their* culture, not ours.

As a result, the Genesis accounts do not fit neatly into our categories of thought. To grasp this point, suppose the first eleven chapters of Genesis were published as a separate book and sent to a library. When the slender volume arrives, the librarian has to decide where to shelve it. First she surveys the nonfiction side of the library. Should it go with works on astronomy? biology? history? On close examination, it seems quite different from modern books on those subjects. Neither does it belong in the psychology section, despite its interesting descriptions of dysfunctional families. The librarian turns to the fiction side of the library. What about shelving the book with collections of short stories? But the Genesis accounts are documents of religious instruction, not imaginative works of art. Finally, exasperated, the librarian considers shelving the book with collections of mythology. Yet the Genesis accounts are different from myths in important respects.

The librarian is puzzled about what kind of book Genesis is because the authors of Genesis combined elements that modern authors keep distinct. The combination of ingredients in Genesis would have been familiar to people in the ancient Near East. But for us modern people, Genesis is virtually unique.

In our experience perhaps the closest parallel to many of the Genesis accounts that we will be reading is the parable. A parable is an imaginative story that communicates a truth and spurs us to think. Jesus delivered much of his teaching through parables. The account of Adam and Eve, for example, is not a historical narrative but a parable-like story that brings out certain meanings. The similarity of Genesis and parables is only partial, however. Parables are pure fiction, but some actual events lie behind the Genesis accounts, even though they are not conveyed in straightforward scientific or historical language.

It is a shame that the parable-like nature of the Genesis accounts was not recognized a couple of centuries ago, for it might have forestalled a lot of unnecessary arguments between advocates of science and advocates of the Bible. Thinking they are defending the Bible against theories that contradict it, many Christians resist evolutionary explanations of the development of species, especially *Homo sapiens.* But the Genesis stories do not aim to convey scientific or historical information. Consequently they cannot be in contradiction of scientific or historical findings. It is apparent, for example, that the narrator of Genesis was not concerned with *how* God brought humans into existence, since he offered different descriptions of the process. Chapter 1 states that God "created" us (1:27), using a Hebrew word that never refers to making one thing from another. Yet chapter 2 says that God "formed" a man from dust and "made" a woman from the man's rib (2:7, 22). Evidently the narrator was intent on communicating *that* God created humans; *how* God did it was not part of the message.

Thus the Genesis account of human creation does not have to be defended against biological theories. Speculating about the processes by which humans developed may be comfortably left to biologists. No biological discoveries can disprove the Genesis message that God created the human race, since in creating us God could have chosen any process that biologists might ever discover.

Parables are very brief. Usually a parable makes only a single point or two. Because of their simplicity, parables raise questions for which there are no answers. Keeping this limitation in mind will save us from asking inappropriate questions as we read Genesis. For example, we may wonder what kind of legs the snake had before God cursed it (3:14) or where Cain's wife came from (4:17) or how Noah and his family coped with the zoo-keeping responsibilities on the ark (7:1–24). These questions are unanswerable for the same reason that there is no answer to questions about how the sheep in Jesus' parable fared after the shepherd left them to look for the stray (Luke 15:3–7). Parables are just not designed to answer questions like that.

Recognizing the parable-like quality of the Genesis accounts keeps us from getting hung up in futile controversies and insoluble questions. This frees us to focus on the meaning of the accounts. The authors of Genesis wrote to shed light on basic questions about human existence. It may be helpful to identify some of those questions before we begin our reading.

Chapter 1 deals particularly with "what" questions:

✦ What is the universe? Most ancient Near Eastern people regarded the universe as a composite formed by three orders of beings: gods who are a part of nature, nature that is filled with gods, and human beings who are dependent on both. In contrast, the account in Genesis 1 elevates God far above nature and strips nature of any divinity.

✦ What is the place of humans in the scheme of things? Ancient people offered various responses: humans are slaves of the gods, playthings of divine forces, intelligent work animals. Because of their worldview, ancient people thought that humans were subject to countless capricious deities and demons, whose favor had to be cultivated and whose ill will had to be warded off. As we will see, Genesis 1 gives a radically different answer to the question.

In chapters 2 and 3, questions of meaning and purpose predominate. For example:

✦ Why is the drive for union between man and woman so strong? What is the meaning of this mystery?

✦ What is the natural status of woman in relation to man?

+ Why are relationships between men and women often marked by shame and exploitation?

+ Why do human beings, who feel so at home in the world, meet such resistance from the natural environment? Why is getting food so hard? Why are animals strangers, even enemies?

+ Why does the great blessing of childbearing involve such pain?

+ Why do we have to die?

+ Why don't snakes have legs? (Not all questions in Genesis are deep, theological ones.)

Key questions in later chapters include the following:

+ In light of the barbaric ways in which humans sometimes treat each other, why doesn't God bring the human race to an end?

+ Why do people, who have such intelligence, often fail to understand each other?

Obviously, these questions concern us too. While Genesis was written in a culture different from ours, it deals with universal human issues. We can grasp the point of Jesus' parables about the kingdom of God, even without knowing a lot about the Galilean fishing and farming that he referred to. Just so, with a little study, we can grasp the basic messages of the Genesis stories without being experts on the ancient Near East.

While the Genesis accounts deal with God's creation of the whole universe, they focus on his relationship with his human creatures. Taken together, the accounts in Genesis 1–11 create contrasting portraits of God and humans. God emerges as a lover of good, a patient judge, a fatherly figure who wants what is best for his human children and is willing to make a new start with them when they mess up. Humans, on the other hand, show themselves to be a mixture of nobility and vice. They are intelligent and creative, capable of doing right, but inclined to transgress their creaturely limits and fatally attracted to the mirage of autonomy from God.

The early chapters of Genesis were the outcome of a long development process, and they have been the subject of centuries of interpretation in Israel and the Church. Reading these accounts at the beginning of the twenty-first century, we are heirs of a tradition of writing and interpretation that stretches back more than three thousand years. Having some notion of this tradition is useful for understanding the accounts and seeing how they apply to us.

By studying the writings of other peoples in the ancient Near East, scholars have come to see that the origins of many Genesis stories go far back, to a period before the formation of Israel (Israel's exodus from Egypt happened around 1250 B.C.). In other words, both the Israelites and their neighbors who did not believe in the God of Israel inherited many of the same mythic descriptions of the beginning of the world from older Near Eastern culture.

Over centuries, as the people of Israel interacted with God, they came to a view of reality different from that of their neighbors. Consequently they reshaped the inherited stories to convey their distinctive picture of God, the world, and human beings. The result was stories that were still similar to those of their neighbors but that now carried new, divinely inspired messages.

The flood story is an example of this process. The Israelites and the Akkadians (in present-day Iraq) both drew on very ancient traditions of a catastrophic flood. In the Akkadian version of the story, the gods bring the flood because people were bothering them with noise. The Israelites, however, had discovered that God is not bad-tempered but just, and they reflected this knowledge in their version of the story. In the biblical telling, God brings the flood because he is saddened by people's violent oppression of each other. In the Israelite tradition, the story became the vehicle for conveying a portrait of a God who is righteous and compassionate, rather than capricious and self-concerned. Thus at one stage the accounts of the beginning served to sketch a truer portrait of God than that held by Israel's neighbors.

The accounts acquired another level of meaning when they were incorporated in the growing book of Scripture. Contrary to what we might expect, the accounts of the beginning were not the

**11**

first part of Genesis to be included in the Bible. The narratives of God's dealings with Abraham and his family and of the exodus from Egypt were composed earlier. Later the accounts of the beginning were placed in front. Joined to the history of God's dealings with Israel, the early accounts now showed that the God who had been unfolding a merciful plan for the people of Israel was not just the tribal God of Israel; he was the God of the whole universe. Thus the Genesis stories implied that God's activity on behalf of Israel must be part of a larger plan for the entire human race.

The Genesis stories reached a third stage of meaning with the coming of Jesus. God achieves his original purposes for the universe through his Son, who has now taken on human nature in Jesus of Nazareth. Since God's creative purposes find their fulfillment in Jesus, the creation accounts in Genesis reveal their deepest meaning when viewed in relation to him. Now that God's Son has come in human flesh, the Genesis accounts provide background against which we can perceive who Jesus is and what he has come to do.

The stories of Adam and Eve, of their sons Cain and Abel, of the people who provoked the flood and those who built the tower of Babel—all these display our human tendency to overstep our creaturely limits, to take control of our lives apart from God, to treat one another unjustly. The Genesis accounts diagnose the human condition: our unhappiness stems from our failure to trust and obey our creator. Against this background, Jesus' life and death emerge as a deliberate reversal of the deep-rooted human tendency to distrust and disobey God. St. Augustine writes that Jesus "did not come to do his own will but the will of God by whom he was sent. In this he differed from Adam who chose to do his own will, not the will of his creator." Jesus' death and resurrection become understandable as the divine means of putting an end to our rebellion—symbolized in the Genesis accounts—in order to give us a fresh start in relationship with God (Romans 6:3–10). Just as Adam was the first human being, through whom we have received our human life flawed by sin, so Jesus is the new Adam, through whom we receive a life cleansed of sin and enlightened by the presence of God's Spirit (Romans 5:12–19; 1 Corinthians 15:21–22, 45).

Given the inner connection between God's initial purposes revealed in Genesis and the fulfillment of those purposes through Jesus, it is not surprising that the early Church drew heavily on the Genesis accounts to help explain Jesus. For example, the early Church viewed the cross on which Jesus died as a "tree" corresponding to the tree in the garden of Eden. At the first tree the human race lost its original relationship with God by distrust and disobedience; it regained this relationship with God through Jesus' trust and obedience at the second tree.

As centuries have passed in the life of the Church, Christians asking questions about God's plan have returned again and again to the Genesis accounts of beginnings. St. Augustine, who died in the early fifth century, investigated Genesis as he tried to understand how there came to be any evil in a universe created by a perfectly good and powerful God. Augustine and later theologians have scrutinized Genesis for help in understanding the destabilizing effects of Adam's and Eve's disobedience (what theologians refer to as original sin) and the means by which these effects are passed from one generation to another. In the late twentieth century, Pope John Paul II intensively explored the account of Adam and Eve to shed light on the relationship between the sexes and on the "nuptial meaning of the body." The author of Genesis did not directly address these subjects, yet Genesis will always be part of Christians' efforts to deal with such issues.

Scripture is the soul of theology, the bishops of Vatican II pointed out. It is meant to be the soul of our own reflections. Just as the greatest Christian thinkers have repeatedly pondered the opening chapters of Genesis, so may we also read and reread them, seeking to understand God's relationship with us and his purpose for our lives. As we read, the Spirit who guided the narrator of Genesis to write will be with us, guiding us to understand and to act, to wonder and to praise.

# LET THERE BE LIGHT!

## Questions to Begin

*15 minutes*
*Use a question or two to get warmed up for the reading.*

**1** For you, this last week has been
❏ ordinary
❏ unusual
❏ boring
❏ great
❏ a time of grace
❏ a week to forget

**2** Describe a memorable beginning in your life. How did it turn out?

**3** If you could make a fresh start in some area of life, what would it be?

## Opening the Bible

*5 minutes*
*Read the passage aloud. Let individuals take turns reading
paragraphs.*

## The Reading: Genesis 1:1–31

### The Universe: Act One, Scene One

1 In the beginning when God created the heavens and the earth, 2 the
earth was a formless void and darkness covered the face of the deep,
while a wind from God swept over the face of the waters. 3 Then God
said, "Let there be light"; and there was light. 4 And God saw that the
light was good; and God separated the light from the darkness. 5 God
called the light Day, and the darkness he called Night. And there was
evening and there was morning, the first day.

6 And God said, "Let there be a dome in the midst of the
waters, and let it separate the waters from the waters." 7 So God
made the dome and separated the waters that were under the dome
from the waters that were above the dome. And it was so. 8 God
called the dome Sky. And there was evening and there was morning,
the second day.

9 And God said, "Let the waters under the sky be gathered
together into one place, and let the dry land appear." And it was so.
10 God called the dry land Earth, and the waters that were gathered
together he called Seas. And God saw that it was good. 11 Then God
said, "Let the earth put forth vegetation: plants yielding seed, and
fruit trees of every kind on earth that bear fruit with the seed in it."
And it was so. 12 The earth brought forth vegetation: plants yielding
seed of every kind, and trees of every kind bearing fruit with the seed
in it. And God saw that it was good. 13 And there was evening and
there was morning, the third day.

### Creatures of Sea, Air, and Land

14 And God said, "Let there be lights in the dome of the sky to
separate the day from the night; and let them be for signs and for
seasons and for days and years, 15 and let them be lights in the dome
of the sky to give light upon the earth." And it was so. 16 God made
the two great lights—the greater light to rule the day and the lesser
light to rule the night—and the stars. 17 God set them in the dome of
the sky to give light upon the earth, 18 to rule over the day and over
the night, and to separate the light from the darkness. And God saw
that it was good. 19 And there was evening and there was morning,
the fourth day.

20 And God said, "Let the waters bring forth swarms of living creatures, and let birds fly above the earth across the dome of the sky." 21 So God created the great sea monsters and every living creature that moves, of every kind, with which the waters swarm, and every winged bird of every kind. And God saw that it was good. 22 God blessed them, saying, "Be fruitful and multiply and fill the waters in the seas, and let birds multiply on the earth." 23 And there was evening and there was morning, the fifth day.

24 And God said, "Let the earth bring forth living creatures of every kind: cattle and creeping things and wild animals of the earth of every kind." And it was so. 25 God made the wild animals of the earth of every kind, and the cattle of every kind, and everything that creeps upon the ground of every kind. And God saw that it was good.

## God's Masterpiece

26 Then God said, "Let us make humankind in our image, according to our likeness; and let them have dominion over the fish of the sea, and over the birds of the air, and over the cattle, and over all the wild animals of the earth, and over every creeping thing that creeps upon the earth."

27 So God created humankind in his image,
    in the image of God he created them;
    male and female he created them.

28 God blessed them, and God said to them, "Be fruitful and multiply, and fill the earth and subdue it; and have dominion over the fish of the sea and over the birds of the air and over every living thing that moves upon the earth." 29 God said, "See, I have given you every plant yielding seed that is upon the face of all the earth, and every tree with seed in its fruit; you shall have them for food. 30 And to every beast of the earth, and to every bird of the air, and to everything that creeps on the earth, everything that has the breath of life, I have given every green plant for food." And it was so. 31 God saw everything that he had made, and indeed, it was very good. And there was evening and there was morning, the sixth day.

**Questions for Careful Reading**

*10 minutes*
*Choose questions according to your interest and time.*

**1** How does God's evaluation of his work in verse 31 differ from his previous evaluations? What might be the significance of this difference?

**2** What are animals and humans given the freedom to eat? By implication, what are they restricted from eating? What might be the significance of this restriction?

**3** What picture of God could be drawn simply on the basis of this reading from Genesis?

**4** Most ancient Near Eastern people thought of the sun, moon, and stars as gods. What would verses 14–18 say about such a belief?

## A Guide to the Reading

*If participants have not read this section already, read it aloud. Otherwise go on to "Questions for Application."*

Picture a movie scene that includes the use of cartoon-type animation. An artist sitting at an easel begins to paint. She sweeps her brush in broad strokes back and forth across the canvas. Through animation, at each stroke objects magically appear. With one stroke of the brush, a tree springs into view. Another stroke and a meadow surrounds the tree. Two dabs of the brush put a sun in the sky and a child beneath the tree. Suddenly the picture comes to life. The tree's branches sway in the breeze. The child runs across the meadow.

Genesis 1 is like that. God calls forth the universe in six days, each day an effortless stroke of an artist's brush. The account does not describe the processes by which the universe took shape and life developed, any more than the animation shows how an artist actually paints a picture. But Genesis teaches us things we cannot learn from astronomy or biology.

A narrator must say when and where the action begins. This requirement poses a problem. Before creation there *was* no time or place. Nothing had been created. Yet verse 3 cannot stand as the beginning of the account, so the narrator describes the "situation" before creation: a shapeless emptiness, a watery darkness whipped by storms (verse 2; "wind from God" is probably a Hebrew way of describing an extremely violent wind). The narrator describes what cannot really be described, because it did not exist. (While Genesis probably had several authors and editors, for the sake of simplicity I will refer to "the narrator" or "the author" in this booklet.)

The author does not describe creation from nothing in quite the way that later theologians have come to understand it. Yet neither does he say that anything existed before God created. When the author describes God performing operations on the watery darkness (1:6–10), he does not mean that God formed the world out of preexisting matter, for the dark ocean of verse 2 is not neutral matter in our modern sense. It is chaos, sinister nothingness, absence of any possibility of life. The account of God's illuminating darkness and dividing waters (1:3–10) is a way of conveying that God called into existence an orderly universe.

It seems strange that God creates light on the first day, while sun and stars appear only on the fourth, but the narrator is pursuing a logic of his own. The purpose of the light is to inaugurate time, as indicated by the naming of what is created: "Day" and "Night" (1:5). Next God creates space. He establishes vertical space by engineering the sky, which ancient people thought of as a hard, transparent dome holding up a vast, blue ocean (1:6–8). God makes horizontal space by clearing away water to expose the land (1:9–10).

Calling earth "Earth" and seas "Seas" (1:10) seems an exercise in the obvious. But in the culture of the time, name-giving indicated possession (see Isaiah 43:1). Thus the account shows that the universe is God's property; it belongs to him. Notice that God does not name the animals (keep this in mind for next week).

After creating various creatures (1:20–25), God reaches the climax of his efforts. Here he does not merely utter a "Let there be." God deliberates with himself—"Let us make" (1:26)—carefully considering his greatest undertaking.

God creates humans in his "image" and "likeness" (1:26–27). In the ancient Near East, kings were considered images of the gods. Thus for humans to be made in the image of God means, as scholar Nahum M. Sarna says, that "each person bears the stamp of royalty." God has made us with the intelligence and freedom required to carry out a royal assignment. God assigns us as his viceroys to govern the earth and its creatures (1:26).

Being made in God's image means even more than this, for it also means that we *correspond* to God. We are made like God in order to interact with him. There is a fit, a match, between God and us that makes a relationship possible. Scholar Claus Westermann writes, "The creation of humanity has as its goal a happening between God and human beings." In our entire physical and spiritual nature we are created for a relationship with God. As soon as the first human couple stands before him, God activates this relationship. We read for the first time, "God said to them" (1:28). Among earth's creatures, with humanity alone can God carry on a conversation.

## Questions for Application

*40 minutes*
*Choose questions according to your interest and time.*

**1**  Where is there disorder, disintegration, or absurdity in your life? What are the dangers and threats posed to you and those you are close to? Where do you long to see God bring order, peace, and protection? What effect can this week's reading have on your trust in God in these areas?

**2**  What difference should knowing that the universe belongs to God make in how we treat the earth? If you were to consider the tiny part of creation that God has put in your hands as his personal possession—your house, your car, your bank account, your yard, your dog— how might you relate to it differently?

**3**  What might this week's reading say about the belief that the movements of the stars and planets determine the course of people's lives?

**4** When have you become particularly aware that God is seeking a personal relationship with you? What do you intend to do to respond more fully to his invitation?

**5** God gives the whole human race the mandate to "be fruitful and multiply, and fill the earth" (1:28). How could parents and those who are not parents work together more effectively to foster the development of the children God has given your church community?

**"Clarifying the members' motivations and expectations early in the life of the group saves you from countless aggravations."**

Neal F. McBride, *How to Lead Small Groups*

## Approach to Prayer

*15 minutes*
*Use this approach — or create your own!*

---

✦   Now that you have read the repeated divine declarations that "it is good," it is your turn to reflect them back to God in a litany of thanks:

First recite Genesis 1:31 together: "God saw everything that he had made, and indeed, it was very good."

Then allow participants to mention things for which they are grateful, pausing after each item for the group to pray together, "Thank you, Lord, for the goodness of your creation."

Recite Genesis 1:31 together again, and close by praying Psalm 8.

**Saints in the Making**

*God and Our Chaos*

*This section is a supplement for individual reading.*

G enesis 1 depicts creation as an ordering of chaos. God shatters the darkness of nonexistence by creating light, then joins darkness as a subordinate to the light in the alternating rhythm of night and day (1:1–5). God rolls back the life-negating deep; assigned now to a place beside the land, the tamed waters become the bright sea (1:6–10).

While God imposes order on chaos, tendencies to disintegration and absurdity are not entirely eliminated from creation. In the Israelite view, night and ocean continue as zones of danger, symbols of the destruction that lurks at the edges of life. Creation constantly needs the creator to keep bringing the dawn, to keep holding back the floodwaters from the dry land.

The sense that life is not a neat, ordered whole is probably common to all of us. Bernadette McCarver Snyder suggests that chaos is as near as the kitchen sink. "For many of us across the land," she writes, "the dawn does not come up like thunder. It comes up with the rattle of dirty dishes. No matter how late you stay up sanitizing the kitchen at night, the next morning there will be DIRTY DISHES somewhere. Either they regenerate themselves, or somebody up there wants me to have dishpan hands."

With a little self-knowledge, we recognize that disorder is within as well as without. Dom Helder Camara, bishop of Recife, Brazil, told an interviewer, "At two in the morning, I always wake up, get up, get dressed, and gather up the pieces I've scattered during the day—an arm here, a leg there, the head who knows where. I sew myself back together again; all alone, I start thinking or writing or praying, or I get ready for Mass."

At times, the hammer blows of loss smash our lives into meaningless fragments. Antoinette Bosco writes, "Divorce made me yearn for the miracle of reconnection, the gift of being able to pick up the pieces of a shattered life and build a new, radically different one."

At every stage of our journey, the Genesis image of a chaos-ordering God stands before us as a sign of hope. The God who spoke light into being, who divided water and land to make a beautiful world, is with us each day as we make our way toward wholeness in his presence.

# *Between* Discussions

L et's suppose that friends from New Jersey have come to visit me in Minnesota, where I live, and they ask me about the state. In response I tell them about the Twin Cities, the Scandinavian background of many Minnesotans, the Vikings football team, and the Mall of America. My East Coast friends might not notice, but if I stopped there, my list would lack some pretty obvious features of life in Minnesota. Any of my Minnesota neighbors who were listening would wonder why, for example, I hadn't mentioned fishing, since virtually all Minnesotans love to fish, no matter what city they live in, what country their ancestors came from, what teams they support, or where they shop. And how could I have forgotten to say something about our Siberian winters?

We modern readers may not immediately notice, but the narrator of Genesis has also left out some features that his non-Israelite neighbors would have expected in a creation account. Most notably he has purged his account of any notion of a multiplicity of gods.

Many ancient Near Eastern people imagined that the world came into existence as the result of a battle between gods. They tended to think of creation as a laborious process in which gods made some things from other things. Genesis 1 has none of this. God creates without needing to overcome the opposition of other deities because, quite simply, there aren't any. He summons things into existence instantly by mere command.

In one ancient creation myth, a certain god slays another god, called Sea, who has the form of a sea monster, and uses the corpse to construct the world. The author of Genesis knew this story—and rejected it. In Genesis the sea is not divine; the "deep" in 1:2 is simply an image of chaos, of nonbeing. The sea does not emerge until the third day (1:9–10) and is merely an element of creation. Sea monsters are just the biggest, oddest pets in God's global aquarium (1:21).

Ancient readers would have been struck especially by the Genesis narrator's treatment of the sun, moon, and other heavenly bodies (1:14–18). Near Eastern people saw these things as gods who ruled human lives. Genesis 1 firmly demotes them from divine status. First, God creates them. Second, they do not appear until the fourth day. They have no light of their own but merely transmit light already created (1:3). They serve to mark the passage of time and the occurrence of holidays (1:14); that is all. Far from being gods, they are nonentities: they do not even have names (see 1:16).

Writing in a period when people conceived of a universe crowded with conflicting divine beings, the narrator of Genesis offered a simpler, yet deeper, view: one God has created all. This God is not a power *within* the universe—a power of sun or sea or storm or sex. He is *the* power that has brought every other power into existence. Therefore we humans should worship, revere, listen to, and love this God alone. There is no need to worry about pleasing or placating any other gods.

In many places in the world, this is a very relevant, up-to-date, and countercultural message. Think of India, for example. But what about we who live in Western societies? Our public spaces and institutions are secularized. We do not meet statues of gods in schools or supermarkets or courtrooms. In our society, people look for scientific, rather than mythic, explanations of the origin of things. On the other hand, many people in our society believe that human lives may be influenced by stars, by magic, by supernatural beings of various kinds, by spiritual forces working through places or crystals, by the minds of the dead channeled through human teachers.

Genesis 1, then, carries a twofold message for us. First, in the face of burgeoning beliefs in manifold spiritual powers, Genesis declares absolutely that God is the only deity in the universe. From top to bottom, the universe is God's creation, inhabited only with the creatures that God has put there. Second, as we conduct our lives in secularized settings—in business, in recreation, in government—Genesis reminds us that no time or place exists apart from God. The universe is not meaningless matter; time is not an emptiness filled only with human sound and fury. All places and times, and we ourselves, are the handiwork and possession of a personal God.

# THE FIRST MARRIAGE

## Questions to Begin

*15 minutes*
*Use a question or two to get warmed up for the reading.*

**1** What's the nicest place you've ever lived in or visited? What did you like about it?

**2** What is the best job you've ever had? If you could design the perfect job for yourself, what would it be?

*Read the passage aloud. Let individuals take turns reading paragraphs. (If participants have not already read "What's Happened," read that aloud also. Otherwise skip it.)*

## What's Happened

God completes his six days of creation with a day of rest (2:1–3). But the narrator has not said everything he wishes about the creation of the human race in chapter 1, so he continues with a second account. The first account highlights humans' exalted status by setting our creation last: we are the summit of creation. The second account makes the same point in the opposite way, by placing the creation of humans before that of other living things. The first account indicates that we are made for a relationship with God by saying that we are in his image and likeness. The second account makes this point by showing the personal care with which God fashions and breathes life into man and woman.

## The Reading: Genesis 2:4–25

The First Man

4 These are the generations of the heavens and the earth when they were created.

In the day that the LORD God made the earth and the heavens, 5 when no plant of the field was yet in the earth and no herb of the field had yet sprung up—for the LORD God had not caused it to rain upon the earth, and there was no one to till the ground; 6 but a stream would rise from the earth, and water the whole face of the ground— 7 then the LORD God formed man from the dust of the ground,* and breathed into his nostrils the breath of life; and the man became a living being. 8 And the LORD God planted a garden in Eden, in the east; and there he put the man whom he had formed. 9 Out of the ground the LORD God made to grow every tree that is pleasant to the sight and good for food, the tree of life also in the midst of the garden, and the tree of the knowledge of good and evil.

* The Hebrew word for man/mankind/human being *(adam)* sounds like the word for ground *(adamah)*.

¹⁰ A river flows out of Eden to water the garden, and from there it divides and becomes four branches. ¹¹ The name of the first is Pishon; it is the one that flows around the whole land of Havilah, where there is gold; ¹² and the gold of that land is good; bdellium and onyx stone are there. ¹³ The name of the second river is Gihon; it is the one that flows around the whole land of Cush. ¹⁴ The name of the third river is Tigris, which flows east of Assyria. And the fourth river is the Euphrates.

## Madam, I'm Adam

¹⁵ The LORD God took the man and put him in the garden of Eden to till it and keep it. ¹⁶ And the LORD God commanded the man, "You may freely eat of every tree of the garden; ¹⁷ but of the tree of the knowledge of good and evil you shall not eat, for in the day that you eat of it you shall die."

¹⁸ Then the LORD God said, "It is not good that the man should be alone; I will make him a helper as his partner." ¹⁹ So out of the ground the LORD God formed every animal of the field and every bird of the air, and brought them to the man to see what he would call them; and whatever the man called every living creature, that was its name. ²⁰ The man gave names to all cattle, and to the birds of the air, and to every animal of the field; but for the man there was not found a helper as his partner. ²¹ So the LORD God caused a deep sleep to fall upon the man, and he slept; then he took one of his ribs and closed up its place with flesh. ²² And the rib that the LORD God had taken from the man he made into a woman and brought her to the man. ²³ Then the man said,

"This at last is bone of my bones
and flesh of my flesh;
this one shall be called Woman,
for out of Man this one was taken."*

²⁴ Therefore a man leaves his father and his mother and clings to his wife, and they become one flesh. ²⁵ And the man and his wife were both naked, and were not ashamed.

* The Hebrew word for woman (ishshah) sounds like the word for man/adult male (ish).

*10 minutes*
*Choose questions according to your interest and time.*

**1** In chapter 1 God gives names to the basic components of the world. In chapter 2 the man names the living creatures. What does this tell us about human beings?

**2** What do verses 8–9 and 19–20 suggest about God's purpose for the plants and animals on the earth?

**3** Verses 23 and 24 are linked by the word *therefore*. What is the narrator trying to explain? How would you clarify the explanation to someone who asked your help in understanding it?

**4** How is the creation account in chapter 2 different from the account in chapter 1? What different points do the two accounts emphasize? Do the two accounts give a somewhat different picture of God?

## A Guide to the Reading

*If participants have not read this section already, read it aloud. Otherwise go on to "Questions for Application."*

God forms a human being from the ground (2:7). The narrator does not encourage us to picture the manner in which God creates the first human. The account does not speak of God literally using hands to mold the human figure. The man is formed from dust—hardly suitable material for molding. The actual process of human creation is left shrouded in mystery.

The account stresses the lofty dignity of human beings. Even though we consist of ordinary material elements, we have received our life directly from God. He has brought us into existence in, and for, a face-to-face relationship with him (2:7).

God plants an orchard to nourish the man (2:8–9). Eden is not a resort: the man is assigned to take care of it (2:15). "Work was man's sober destiny even in his original state," scholar Gerhard von Rad observes. Exercising "dominion" over the earth (1:26) requires effort. But of itself work is a gift, not a curse.

Two trees stand out (2:9). One is the tree of life. Apparently humans were not made immune to death. We needed something to sustain our lives. God intended that we would not die, but this was to be accomplished through eating the fruit of the tree of life. St. Augustine regards this tree as a kind of sacrament. "By an invisible power from the visible tree of life," he writes, humans would draw strength, until eventually God transformed them and, without death, enabled them to enter heaven.

We will leave the discussion of the tree of the knowledge of good and evil until next week. Clearly, however, being forbidden to eat its fruit is a limitation imposed on the man. It represents the reality that to be a creature is inevitably to have limits. Yet God is not preoccupied with limits. He gives the man work; he grants him broad freedom in picking fruit (2:15–16). God is not predominantly a naysayer. Unfortunately, as scholar Walter Brueggemann writes, "in the popular understanding of this story, little attention is given the mandate of *vocation* or the gift of *permission. . . .* The God of the garden is chiefly remembered as the one who *prohibits.*"

Alone the man cannot live a truly human life. He needs community. God wishes him to have "a helper as his partner" (2:18). The Hebrew word translated "helper" is not a servant word like *waiter* or *caterer.* It simply means "help." Usually it refers to God or God's help, as in Psalm 121:1–2: "I lift up my eyes to the hills— from where will my *help* come? My *help* comes from the LORD, who made heaven and earth" (italics mine).

God wants the man to have a helper "as his partner," or "corresponding to him." Together the words *help* and *partner* could be rendered "a helper who is his true counterpart." Sexual complementarity is implied. God envisions a companion for the man in facing the practical necessities of life (a helper), not just now and then but throughout life, since this companion will be joined to him as a spouse (his true counterpart).

Searching for such a creature, God makes animals and brings them to the man to see if any of them might serve as a partner (who says there's no humor in the Bible?). By naming the animals the man completes the name-giving that God left unfinished in chapter 1, thus beginning to fulfill humans' role as God's representative. But none of the animals is an appropriate life companion for the man (2:19–20).

Most of the Genesis accounts are similar to stories told by Israel's neighbors. But 2:18–24 is the only account of the creation of woman known from the ancient Near East. The story expresses a high valuation of women: woman, taken from man, is man's equal.

The image of woman taken from man speaks about man's and woman's deep-rooted drive for union with each other. The story indicates that when man and woman are drawn together in marriage, they fulfill the destiny for which God created them. In the ancient world, property and status strongly influenced decisions about who married whom, yet these are not identified here as reasons for marriage. The account puts the accent on man's and woman's attraction to each other, dramatically expressed in the man's delighted recognition of the woman (2:23). Remarkably, not even offspring are mentioned here as a reason for marriage (that was covered in 1:28). Claus Westermann remarks, "[Verse 24] points to the basic power of love between man and woman"—a power given by God.

## Questions for Application

*40 minutes*
*Choose questions according to your interest and time.*

**1**  When have you been lonely? Is loneliness an inescapable part of life? How can you tell when someone is lonely? Is there someone whose loneliness you could relieve?

**2**  How has work been a blessing for you? In what ways has it been a mixed blessing?

**3**  When has God unexpectedly provided something good for you? What effect has this had on your relationship with him?

**4** Who have been the most important helpers and companions on your journey through life? To whom is God giving you as a helper at this stage in life? What could you do to better show love in these relationships?

**"The leader may be the same person for all the sessions, or the group may decide to rotate leadership."**

Loretta Girzaitis, *Guidebook for Bible Study*

## Approach to Prayer

*15 minutes*
*Use this approach — or create your own!*

---

✦ Pray for those who are married
and those who are lonely (these
are not mutually exclusive
groups).

Let someone pray this prayer
aloud:

*Father, thank you for your plan
for sex and marriage. Thank you
for our marriages and the
marriages of those we know.
Give new grace to all who are
married. Inspire spouses to
respect each other, to appreciate
each other, to be kind to each
other, to find joy in each other.
Help spouses to repent. Protect
them from discouragement.*

Give participants a chance to
offer short, spontaneous prayers
along this line. Then let another
participant pray this prayer:

*Lord, thank you for being the
ultimate helper of our lives. You
are the companion who never
abandons or neglects us. Show
your presence and love to all
those who are lonely.*

End with an Our Father.

*A Saint Who Found Genesis Hard to Understand*

*This section is a supplement for individual reading.*

St. Augustine, a North African bishop who died in 425, was one of the greatest thinkers in the history of the Church. Yet he labored to understand Genesis for more than thirty years and still had questions. Augustine wrote a commentary on Genesis soon after his adult conversion. Dissatisfied, he returned to the challenge of interpretation a few years later but gave up before finishing the book. "I collapsed under the weight of a burden I could not bear," he said later. Eventually Augustine wrote a third commentary. It took him fourteen years.

In his exploration of Genesis, Augustine showed intellectual humility. When it came to the mysteries of how God created the world, Augustine found it easy to "acknowledge that we do not know that which is so far outside our experience." While Augustine offered his own explanation of Genesis, he was open to better interpretations. "If anyone is of the opinion that this passage should be explained differently and he is able to lay out a more likely interpretation," Augustine wrote, "not only should I not resist him, I should thank him."

Keenly aware of the limits of his knowledge, Augustine was wary of arguing too strongly for his own views. At one point he cut short his discussion of a passage, saying, "Let us end here, so that we might maintain moderation in our investigation of Scripture, showing carefulness rather than asserting unfounded opinions."

Augustine did not think that the search for the truth of Genesis could be advanced by noisy debates. "It is better to admit that we are in doubt regarding obscure things than to argue over them. Such things are perhaps just barely discovered by those who seek calmly, never by those striving contentiously."

Not surprisingly, Augustine constantly reminded his readers that God's help is indispensable for understanding Genesis. Augustine said he did not know how much the Lord was going to help him in his commentary, but he knew one thing for sure: "Unless the Lord helps, I am not going to speak rightly!"

It seems that Augustine would have been an ideal participant in any adult discussion of Genesis.

# *Between* Discussions

The hope of eternal happiness with God after earthly life spread gradually among Jews in the Old Testament period. As it did, Jews began to look back to the garden in Eden as an image of final bliss. It seemed reasonable to think that the happiness that God would grant at the end of the world would resemble the happiness he granted at the beginning. In their reflections they sometimes used the term *Paradise*—a Persian word meaning "a walled park of trees"—to refer to Eden and, by extension, to eternal life with God.

As far as we know, in his teaching Jesus did not use Eden as an image of eternal life, but he referred to it at one crucial moment. As he hung on the cross, Jesus assured a man dying next to him, "Today you will be with me in Paradise" (Luke 23:43).

The early Christians continued to consider Eden a glimpse of the happiness of heaven (2 Corinthians 12:1–4). Among those who took up this line of reflection was a fourth-century Syrian deacon named Ephrem. His *Hymns of Paradise* is one of the most beautiful writings of the early Church.

In the hymns, St. Ephrem pictures Eden as a lush park at the top of a mountain—an interpretation modern scholars affirm, for *Eden* means "luxuriant" and the garden seems to have been on a hilltop, from which springwaters rushed down to the rest of the world (2:10–14). In his description of Eden, however, Ephrem also enlarges imaginatively on the text. Ephrem writes about reading Genesis:

> With joy I met Paradise's story,
> quickly read, but rich in appeal.
> As my tongue read the things revealed in the account,
> my mind took flight and soared,
> exploring its marvels in reverent fear.

For Ephrem, the beauty of Eden expresses a key principle: no matter how much effort is involved on our part, the journey to God is fundamentally a matter of our yielding to God's attraction:

> The weariness of the ascent is not in proportion to its height,
> for its beauty joyfully kindles love in those going up to it,
> alluring with its glorious rays,
> sweet with its fragrances.

Ephrem regards the text of Genesis as an invitation to taste the delights of God's love:

I read the beginning of the text aloud and was delighted,
because its lines were prepared for me; their arms spread out—
the first line desired to kiss me, then offered me her companion.
And when I reached the line where the story of Paradise
is written, it lifted me up and thrust me forward
from the heart of the text to the heart of Paradise. . . .

By the lines of the text, as by a bridge, eye and mind
traveled together to the story of Paradise.
I found the bridge and gate of Paradise
in that text; I crossed over and entered it—
my eye remained outside, while my mind entered within—
and I began to roam in what cannot be written.
That is the splendid height, bright, noble, and lovely,
which Scripture calls Eden, height of happiness.

Mentally entering Paradise, Ephrem imagines its beauty:

There I saw the places of the righteous,
sprinkled with scented oils, breathing out fragrances,
plaited with fruits, crowned with flowers.

Study of the biblical text is the starting point for Ephrem's meditation. But as he reads, something happens to him:

Paradise exalted me because I investigated it, enriched me
    because I studied it.
I forgot my poverty, for it intoxicated me with its fragrance.
I became no longer myself, for it delighted me with its variety.
How intoxicated I became there, because there I forgot my sins!

Ephrem's poetry suggests we reread the text of Genesis— and let God stir our mind and heart.

# DISTRUST, DISOBEDIENCE, AND DISMAY

## Questions to Begin

*15 minutes*
*Use a question or two to get warmed up for the reading.*

**1** What types of punishments did your parents use when you were growing up? Were they effective? What are punishments able—and unable—to accomplish with children and adults?

**2** What one limitation on your life would you remove if you could?

*5 minutes*
*Read the passage aloud. Let individuals take turns reading*
*paragraphs.*

## The Reading: Genesis 3:1–24

### Temptation and Fall

1 Now the serpent was more crafty than any other wild animal that the LORD God had made. He said to the woman, "Did God say, 'You shall not eat from any tree in the garden'?" 2 The woman said to the serpent, "We may eat of the fruit of the trees in the garden; 3 but God said, 'You shall not eat of the fruit of the tree that is in the middle of the garden, nor shall you touch it, or you shall die.'" 4 But the serpent said to the woman, "You will not die; 5 for God knows that when you eat of it your eyes will be opened, and you will be like God, knowing good and evil." 6 So when the woman saw that the tree was good for food, and that it was a delight to the eyes, and that the tree was to be desired to make one wise, she took of its fruit and ate; and she also gave some to her husband, who was with her, and he ate. 7 Then the eyes of both were opened, and they knew that they were naked; and they sewed fig leaves together and made loincloths for themselves.

8 They heard the sound of the LORD God walking in the garden at the time of the evening breeze, and the man and his wife hid themselves from the presence of the LORD God among the trees of the garden. 9 But the LORD God called to the man, and said to him, "Where are you?" 10 He said, "I heard the sound of you in the garden, and I was afraid, because I was naked; and I hid myself." 11 He said, "Who told you that you were naked? Have you eaten from the tree of which I commanded you not to eat?" 12 The man said, "The woman whom you gave to be with me, she gave me fruit from the tree, and I ate." 13 Then the LORD God said to the woman, "What is this that you have done?" The woman said, "The serpent tricked me, and I ate." 14 The LORD God said to the serpent,

"Because you have done this,
　　cursed are you among all animals
　　and among all wild creatures;
upon your belly you shall go,
　　and dust you shall eat
　　all the days of your life.
15 I will put enmity between you and the woman,
　　and between your offspring and hers;

he will strike your head,
and you will strike his heel."
16 To the woman he said,
"I will greatly increase your pangs in childbearing;
in pain you shall bring forth children,
yet your desire shall be for your husband,
and he shall rule over you."
17 And to the man he said,
"Because you have listened to the voice of your wife,
and have eaten of the tree
about which I commanded you,
'You shall not eat of it,'
cursed is the ground because of you;
in toil you shall eat of it all the days of your life;
18 thorns and thistles it shall bring forth for you;
and you shall eat the plants of the field.
19 By the sweat of your face
you shall eat bread
until you return to the ground,
for out of it you were taken;
you are dust,
and to dust you shall return."

20 The man named his wife Eve,* because she was the mother of all living. 21 And the LORD God made garments of skins for the man and for his wife, and clothed them.

22 Then the LORD God said, "See, the man has become like one of us, knowing good and evil; and now, he might reach out his hand and take also from the tree of life, and eat, and live forever"— 23 therefore the LORD God sent him forth from the garden of Eden, to till the ground from which he was taken. 24 He drove out the man; and at the east of the garden of Eden he placed the cherubim, and a sword flaming and turning to guard the way to the tree of life.

* In Hebrew, Eve's name resembles the word for living.

*10 minutes*
*Choose questions according to your interest and time.*

**1** Compare what God says in 2:16–17 with the snake's quotation in 3:1. How does the snake misquote God? What is the effect of the snake's misquotation?

**2** The woman does not quote God exactly, either (3:3). What does she add? What effect does her addition have on the picture of God that she conveys?

**3** Why would the woman believe what the snake says in 3:4–5?

**4** Verse 6 describes how the fruit of the tree of the knowledge of good and evil appears to Eve. How is this fruit different from the fruit of the other trees (see 2:9)? If the fruit of the other trees is also pleasant and nutritious, why is Eve now especially attracted to this one?

## A Guide to the Reading

*If participants have not read this section already, read it aloud.*
*Otherwise go on to "Questions for Application."*

The first puzzle in this reading is the snake. No explanation is provided for how an adversary of God got into the garden or why it misleads the woman. The narrator does not make the snake the focus of attention, probably to avoid shifting the responsibility for disobeying God away from the man and woman.

A greater puzzle is the tree "in the middle of the garden" (3:3)—the tree of the knowledge of good and evil. What does it mean? Clement of Alexandria, a second-century Christian teacher, surmises that the "knowledge of good and evil" represents sexual intercourse. St. Augustine dismisses this line of reasoning, since there was nothing to forbid the man and the woman from having intercourse if they wished. ("Maybe they had to wait for the bride to be given away by her father?" Augustine asks sarcastically. "Or for the appraisal of the dowry?") Some have proposed that the tree represents the ability to distinguish right from wrong. But God's instruction (2:17) assumes that the man and the woman can already grasp that it is wrong to eat the fruit.

Later God says that he himself possesses the knowledge of good and evil (3:22), so this knowledge cannot be inherently sinful but must be inappropriate for human beings. Apparently it means making one's own independent judgments about what will be helpful or harmful for oneself. Eating from this tree represents taking mastery over one's own life—a mastery that rightfully belongs to God. That is why the snake says that eating the fruit makes a person "like God" (3:5): it gives one "a divine and unbridled ability to master one's existence," in the words of Claus Westermann.

The woman sees that the fruit is "good" (3:6). What irony! The *creator* knows what is good and has provided it for human beings (1:4, 31; 2:18), but now the woman decides for herself what is good, against the creator's instructions. She sees that the fruit will make her "wise"; the Hebrew could also be translated "successful." The woman thinks that if she eats the fruit she will know how to run her own life successfully apart from God. What folly!

The woman hands the fruit to her husband, who is "with her" (3:6). Apparently he has been silently present throughout the conversation. The narrator does not report any attempt by the woman to persuade her husband. Perhaps he has reached his own decision to eat the fruit, based on what he has heard the snake say.

Before eating the fruit, the couple cannot fully understand why it is forbidden. Receiving a command that cannot be fully understood raises the issue of trust. A person keeps such a command only because he or she hears in it the voice of the one who commands. God's command gives the first humans the opportunity to trust him. They choose instead to suspect that he does not have their best interests at heart. This lack of trust in God, with the claim to be master of one's own life apart from God, is the root of sin. Uprooting it will require a perfect act of trust in God, a total abandonment of self to God: Jesus' death on a cross.

Eating the fruit shatters the harmony between man and woman and between the couple and God (3:7–8). This is the origin of the moral disorder and broken relationship with God that we are born into—the condition called original sin.

Because the woman and the man have turned away from their creator, the source of life, their lives are poisoned at the source. The woman's source is the man. Now her relationship with him, in which she should experience peace and fulfillment, will be marred by oppression (3:16). The man's source is the ground. Now this relationship is also disturbed: farming will involve back-breaking toil (3:17–19). Significantly the same Hebrew word is used for the woman's pain in childbirth and the man's pain in his work. Adam and Eve suffer different, but equal, penalties.

Regarding the tree of the knowledge of good and evil, God had warned, "In the day that you eat of it you shall die" (2:17)—a statement in the form of a death sentence, equivalent to "You will surely be put to death." Eating the fruit was a capital offense. Now that the man and the woman have violated their relationship with God, God seals off the tree of life (3:22–24). The man and the woman no longer have access to the divine power that would have preserved them against the forces of disintegration. Eventually they will die.

## Questions for Application

*40 minutes*
*Choose questions according to your interest and time.*

---

**1** Has something ever become more attractive or interesting to you because it was forbidden? What did you do? What did you learn?

---

**2** Describe a situation in which a temptation seemed attractive and reasonable at the time but later was shown not to have made as much sense as you had thought.

---

**3** Who do you tend to blame for your sins?

**4** When have you faced a moral choice in which it was crucial to trust that God had your best interests at heart?

**5** When do you find it most difficult to trust in God's care for you? What can you do to express your trust in him?

**"If you disagree with someone else's comments, gently say so. Then explain your point of view from the passage before you."**

Christian Basics Bible Studies series

## Approach to Prayer

*15 minutes*
*Use this approach — or create your own!*

✦ Express your desire not to
follow our first parents in their
distrust and disobedience
toward God. Pray two psalms
that express trust in God:
Psalm 90 and Psalm 131. In an
encounter with Satan, Jesus
exemplified the absolute trust
in God that Psalm 90 speaks of
(Luke 4:9–13). Psalm 131 gives
voice to childlike trust in God
and an acceptance of creaturely
limitations.

**A Living Tradition**

*What Sort of Judge?*

*This section is a supplement for individual reading.*

What picture of God do you get from Genesis 3? A picture of a harsh judge? Around the year 385 St. John Chrysostom gave a series of talks on Genesis in the cathedral parish in Antioch (present-day south central Turkey). John encouraged the laypeople who came to study the Bible with him to see a tenderhearted God in Genesis 3.

John compared God to "an affectionate father who sees his own child dragged down from respectability to the most squalid circumstances by carelessly doing things that are unworthy of his noble birth. Out of warmhearted, fatherly compassion he cannot bear to let his child remain in that condition but wishes to free him from his squalor little by little and bring him back to his original honor." Thus, John said, when Adam and Eve sin, God wastes no time. That very afternoon he goes looking for them in the garden (3:8), with the haste of a physician who makes a house call to a patient needing urgent medical attention.

In John's day judges would not directly address the accused in court. What a contrast with God, who calls directly to Adam (3:9). John surmised that Adam is tongue-tied in his shame, yet God gives him the opportunity to explain himself (3:11). "See the Lord's love for humans, his extravagant forbearance. He is able to punish such a great sinner at once. But he patiently restrains himself and asks him questions, virtually inviting a defense." It seemed to John that God brings his charge of disobedience against Adam as kindly as "a friend speaking with a friend." To John, God seems more disappointed than angry. He imagined God saying to Adam, "Surely I didn't cramp your enjoyment? Didn't I provide you with abundance and put you in charge of everything in Paradise? Didn't I command you to keep away from just this *one* thing?"

Certainly God imposes penalties on Adam and Eve, John acknowledged. But even here God's mercy is evident. God softens the woman's punishment—pain in childbirth—with the joy of the baby who follows. And God has a constructive purpose for the man's punishment: difficulties in his work will function as a helpful reminder that in the future he should humble himself before God and not disregard the creaturely limits God has set for him.

# *Between* Discussions

If you ever pass through Jericho, a city near the Jordan River, be sure to see the *tel*. A tel is an artificial hill consisting of layer upon layer of ruins. A tel was produced in ancient times as one group of people after another lived on a site. Each group would level the buildings of the previous one and build on top. Over the course of centuries, as new levels were added, the town would rise higher and higher. The result is an archaeological wedding cake composed of layers from successive periods. The tel in Jericho is remarkable because Jericho is the longest continuously occupied human site in the world. Looking down a shaft cut through the tel, you can see walls constructed more than nine thousand years ago.

We might compare the Bible to a tel. The levels of the biblical tel are composed not of ruined buildings but of layers of meaning, built up through stages of composition and interpretation. The biblical tel contains many levels of meaning, since the Bible passed through many centuries of writing and editing, then through more centuries of study and reflection.

An example of the multileveled meaning of the Genesis text is the least-appealing participant in the drama of chapter 3: the snake. Over more than three thousand years, the snake has passed through at least five stages of understanding, making it a richly meaningful, while always unpleasant, character.

At the bottom layer of the tel, so to speak, are pre-Israelite myths—stories of origin bearing a religious meaning. Just as the Israelites built their cities on the sites of preexisting Canaanite towns, they also took elements of their religion from older sources. At the pre-Israelite level, ancient Near Eastern people regarded snakes with both awe and dread. The Egyptians put carvings of snakes on the pharaoh's crown, as an expression of divine protection. In various tales, snakes symbolized divine and demonic powers.

The Israelite author provided the next level of meaning. He drew elements from stories of the older, polytheistic culture to weave his accounts of creation and fall. But the narrator campaigned *against* the idea that snakes are divine or demonic. He emphasized that snakes are simply snakes. The nondivine status of the snake is communicated by the statement that it is one of the animals "that the LORD God had made" (3:1). The snake has no spiritual power; it is merely clever. The Genesis narrator wanted his readers to see that there is only one God, who has created everything; the world is not filled with a myriad of deities. The snake's subordinate role in the story underlines the message that humans' unhappiness is brought on not by mean-spirited gods or demons, as Israel's neighbors thought, but by bad choices.

A further level of meaning developed among Jews in the century or so before Christ. They came to a larger understanding of the role of angels in the world, and they also saw that some angels had refused to serve God's purposes. The leader of these rebellious spirits, called the devil, then sought to disrupt God's relationship with his human creatures. Rereading the Genesis account, these Jewish thinkers recognized the snake as a mouthpiece for this leader in his diabolical attempt to bring humans to ruin (Wisdom 2:24).

To this view Christians added their belief that Christ has now overcome the devil by his death and resurrection. In God's declaration that there would be hostility between the offspring of the snake and the offspring of the woman (3:15), Christians detected the first hint that God's Son, born as a human being, would break the grip of the devil over human beings.

More recently an additional layer of meaning has developed. From a modern psychology, the snake might be seen as a symbol of some of our darker unconscious drives. The conversation between the snake and the woman might be read as an expression of an inner dialogue, in which a person's egotistical desires confront the consciousness of moral demands.

While the levels of meaning in the Bible resemble a tel, they are unlike a tel in an important respect. People lived only on the top level of the tel. At each stage, the previous levels lay hidden and inaccessible. This is not the case, however, with the Bible. We can understand, appreciate, and learn from all the levels of meaning that have accumulated in the course of its composition and use. We are the heirs of a rich tradition, a tradition guided by God in both its writing and its interpretation.

# EAST OF EDEN

## Questions to Begin

*15 minutes*
*Use a question or two to get warmed up for the reading.*

**1**   If you made a list of technological innovations you
especially appreciate, what
would you put at the top
of the list?

**2**   What are the advantages
of having children when you
are young? What are the
advantages of having children
when you are older?

*5 minutes*
*Read the passage aloud. Let individuals take turns reading*
*paragraphs.*

## The Reading: Genesis 4:1–5:5

### Envy, Murder, and Judgment

[1] Now the man knew his wife Eve, and she conceived and bore Cain, saying, "I have produced a man with the help of the LORD." [2] Next she bore his brother Abel. Now Abel was a keeper of sheep, and Cain a tiller of the ground. [3] In the course of time Cain brought to the LORD an offering of the fruit of the ground, [4] and Abel for his part brought of the firstlings of his flock, their fat portions. And the LORD had regard for Abel and his offering, [5] but for Cain and his offering he had no regard. So Cain was very angry, and his countenance fell. [6] The LORD said to Cain, "Why are you angry, and why has your countenance fallen? [7] If you do well, will you not be accepted? And if you do not do well, sin is lurking at the door; its desire is for you, but you must master it."

[8] Cain said to his brother Abel, "Let us go out to the field." And when they were in the field, Cain rose up against his brother Abel, and killed him. [9] Then the LORD said to Cain, "Where is your brother Abel?" He said, "I do not know; am I my brother's keeper?" [10] And the LORD said, "What have you done? Listen; your brother's blood is crying out to me from the ground! [11] And now you are cursed from the ground, which has opened its mouth to receive your brother's blood from your hand. [12] When you till the ground, it will no longer yield to you its strength; you will be a fugitive and a wanderer on the earth." [13] Cain said to the LORD, "My punishment is greater than I can bear! [14] Today you have driven me away from the soil, and I shall be hidden from your face; I shall be a fugitive and a wanderer on the earth, and anyone who meets me may kill me." [15] Then the LORD said to him, "Not so! Whoever kills Cain will suffer a sevenfold vengeance." And the LORD put a mark on Cain, so that no one who came upon him would kill him. [16] Then Cain went away from the presence of the LORD, and settled in the land of Nod, east of Eden.

### A Clever but Ruthless Family

[17] Cain knew his wife, and she conceived and bore Enoch; and he built a city, and named it Enoch after his son Enoch. [18] To Enoch was born Irad; and Irad was the father of Mehujael, and Mehujael the

father of Methushael, and Methushael the father of Lamech.

19 Lamech took two wives; the name of the one was Adah, and the name of the other Zillah. 20 Adah bore Jabal; he was the ancestor of those who live in tents and have livestock. 21 His brother's name was Jubal; he was the ancestor of all those who play the lyre and pipe. 22 Zillah bore Tubal-cain, who made all kinds of bronze and iron tools. The sister of Tubal-cain was Naamah.

23 Lamech said to his wives:

"Adah and Zillah, hear my voice;
    you wives of Lamech, listen to what I say:
I have killed a man for wounding me,
    a young man for striking me.
24 If Cain is avenged sevenfold,
    truly Lamech seventy-sevenfold."

## Adam and Eve Carry On

25 Adam knew his wife again, and she bore a son and named him Seth, for she said, "God has appointed for me another child instead of Abel, because Cain killed him." 26 To Seth also a son was born, and he named him Enosh. At that time people began to invoke the name of the LORD.

5:1 This is the list of the descendants of Adam. When God created humankind, he made them in the likeness of God. 2 Male and female he created them, and he blessed them and named them "Humankind" when they were created.

3 When Adam had lived one hundred thirty years, he became the father of a son in his likeness, according to his image, and named him Seth. 4 The days of Adam after he became the father of Seth were eight hundred years; and he had other sons and daughters. 5 Thus all the days that Adam lived were nine hundred thirty years; and he died.

## Questions for Careful Reading

*10 minutes*
*Choose questions according to your interest and time.*

**1** How does Cain's response to God (4:9) compare to his father's response (3:10, 12)? How is Cain like his father? How is he different?

**2** Reread 3:21 and 4:15. What do they suggest about God's relationship with sinners?

**3** Cain does not express repentance. Neither do Adam and Eve. Why?

**4** Compare 3:2–6 and 4:6–8. How does the narrator show that Adam and Eve and Cain were responsible for their actions?

**5** What do Jesus' words in Matthew 18:21–22 suggest about his view of Lamech's words in Genesis 4:23–24?

## A Guide to the Reading

*If participants have not read this section already, read it aloud. Otherwise go on to "Questions for Application."*

Adam and Eve have intercourse, and Eve bears a son (4:1). Eve declares that she has "produced" a man with the help of the Lord; the Hebrew word may be translated "created" (as in Proverbs 8:22). Despite their banishment from the garden of Eden, in begetting new human beings, man and woman are cocreators with God—an awesome privilege. Eve calls God "the LORD," using God's proper name in the Old Testament (Hebrew "Yahweh"). Notably it is a woman who first utters this name, so sacred in Jewish tradition that later it came almost never to be spoken.

Conflict arises between the first two brothers when God accepts Abel's offering but not Cain's (4:3–5). The narrator does not tell us why God rejects Cain's offering. Perhaps Cain has done something wrong. Or this may be the first of many biblical episodes in which God, for reasons known only to him, favors a younger son over an older one (for example, Joseph over his brothers—Genesis 37:1–11). The acceptance of Abel's offering and the rejection of Cain's may thus represent situations where inexplicable inequality exists between people. Cain is an everyman, tempted, as we all are, to envy God's apparently more favorable treatment of someone else.

God compares Cain's temptation to a beast crouching to spring (4:7)—a vivid image of the destructive power of envy and rage. We have been created to rule the world (1:28), but we must first decide whether to rule ourselves.

Cain chooses not to. Consequently the first death comes not from natural causes but by human hands. Nahum M. Sarna notes, "Man and woman had striven to gain immortality, but their first-born brings the reality of death into the world." In response, God imposes a severe penalty (4:12): ancient people felt banishment to be as harsh a punishment as death.

Cain protests. Sensing that God is compassionate, Cain describes the suffering that he foresees, hoping God will be moved to lighten the sentence (4:13–14). This appeal is the first prayer of petition in the Bible, made by a man guilty of murder, and God hears it! Thus the episode contains both the cry of Abel's blood and the lament of his killer, and neither goes unheeded. Claus Westermann comments that no matter what a man's or woman's situation, "the person remains within earshot of the creator."

Driven away from God because of his crime, Cain yet remains in God's care. Cain's life, no less than Abel's, belongs to God. To deter anyone from avenging Abel's murder, God puts a mark on Cain (4:15). Since this mark identifies him as a killer, it is a mark of shame, but chiefly it is a safeguard, showing that God remains Cain's protector. The narrator does not say what the mark is. It may have been a mark on the forehead. Early Jewish rabbis, living in a culture that considered dogs no better than rats, suggested that the mark that God gave Cain was a dog as a companion. (I have a hard time imagining Rupert, my happy-go-lucky Shih-Tzu, in such a grim role.)

Cain and his descendants develop the rudiments of civilization and urban life (4:17–22). The seven generations, from Adam through Cain to Lamech, correspond to the seven days of creation: in our efforts to cultivate and develop the earth, we are coworkers with God, made in his image. The fact that technology is produced by *Cain's* descendants does not diminish its goodness. But God-given intelligence is now being used by a race that often rejects God's purposes.

Cain's descendant Lamech boasts of doing the very thing against which God protected Cain: blood vengeance (4:24). This claim exposes the irrationality of revenge, for if people had done to Lamech's ancestor what Lamech does to his enemies, Cain would have been killed and Lamech would never have existed. The span from Cain to Lamech marks a descent into violence. Yet the race is not utterly corrupt. Brutal Lamech has a daughter called Naamah—a Hebrew name that means "pleasant" or "dear" (4:22). Perhaps her charming mother has something to do with this; *Zillah* may mean "melody" (4:19).

Returning to Adam and Eve, the narrator tells us that they continue to have children, who are also made in the divine image (5:3). Despite our sins, we continue to bear the dignity of being in God's likeness; we continue to exist for the purpose of a relationship with God. Our final verse (5:5) records the tragedy that has befallen Adam and all his descendants: earthly death.

## Questions for Application

*40 minutes*
*Choose questions according to your interest and time.*

**1** Considering the differences in abilities and resources and circumstances between people, is God fair? Is he just?

**2** Whom do you envy? What is wrong with envy? From your own experience, what are the results of envy?

**3** Are there both healthy and unhealthy kinds of anger among family members? How can you tell the difference?

**4** When are you tempted to
misuse the technology that is
at your disposal (machinery,
appliances, electronics)? How
can you overcome this
temptation?

**5** What are the effects of
vengefulness or other kinds of
bitterness? How might you
express forgiveness and love
when you are tempted to feel
vengeful?

**"Discussion proceeds best if there is an atmosphere of mutual
respect but informality."**

John Burke, O.P., *Beginners' Guide to Bible Sharing*

## Approach to Prayer

*15 minutes*
*Use this approach — or create your own!*

---

✦ Pray together this portion of a
prayer by St. Francis of Assisi:

*Lord, make me an instrument
of your peace. Where there is
hatred, let me sow love; where
there is injury, let me sow par-
don. Where there is darkness,
let me give light; where there
is sadness, let me give joy.*

*O divine Master, grant that I
may not try to be comforted, but
to comfort; not try to be loved,
but to love.*

*Because it is in giving that we are
received; it is in forgiving that we
are forgiven; and it is in dying
that we are born to eternal life.*

## Saints in the Making

### *Light over the Scaffold*

*This section is a supplement for individual reading.*

On February 25, 1954, twenty-three-year-old Jacques Fesch beat and robbed an elderly broker in an office in the financial district of Paris. Fesch hoped to buy a boat with the money. When the victim's cries attracted attention, Fesch fled into the street, pursued by a policeman named George Vergnes. After a brief chase, Vergnes closed in on Fesch and shouted to him to surrender. In panic Fesch turned, pulled a gun from his overcoat, and shot Vergnes through the heart, killing him instantly. Fesch was captured minutes later at a nearby subway station.

After interrogation, Fesch was placed in solitary confinement until his trial. The prison chaplain came to see him, but at first Fesch was not interested in talking with him.

In solitude Fesch tried to understand his own actions. The robbery had been his first crime. Fesch began to see himself with great clarity. "During the years when I lived without faith," he wrote, "I did evil, much evil, less through deliberate malice than through heedlessness, egoism, and hardness of heart. I was incapable of loving anyone." Fesch realized that the robbery and murder were the "logical consequence of all the evil seething" within him.

After several months' imprisonment, Fesch had an experience of grace. "A powerful wave of emotion swept over me, causing deep and brutal suffering," he wrote. "Within the space of a few hours I came into possession of faith."

Aided by the prison chaplain, his lawyer, and a monk who wrote to him, the young prisoner began a journey toward God. The investigation, trial, and appeals stretched out for three years from Fesch's conversion to his execution. Alone in his cell, Fesch prayed, read, reflected on his life, and wrote letters, which revealed his repentance and a deepening honesty. Humility began to replace egoism. Fesch told his mother that, corresponding with the monk, "I feel like a raccoon trying to carry on a conversation with a dove in the clouds. . . . If he could ever see into the recesses of my soul!"

In his final letter, written the morning of his execution, he expressed both overwhelming fear and supreme confidence in Christ's promise of forgiveness and eternal life.

# *Between* Discussions

A dam and Eve overstep the limit that God set for them, trying to make themselves masters of their own lives (chapter 3). Chapter 4 shows the unhappy effects of this choice on their children and descendants. From Cain to Lamech, the human race goes from bad to worse.

These early chapters of Genesis also show God holding steady to his purposes in the face of human decline. At the beginning God put the blessing of fertility within us and gave us the capacity to rule the earth (1:28). Eve's exultant cry at the birth of her first child and the technological and artistic creativity of the Cain family (4:1, 20–22) demonstrate that God has not withdrawn his gifts. A picture develops of a persevering God who continues to look for ways to accomplish his purposes with his now deeply flawed, but still deeply loved, human creatures. God generously blesses us with our lives, our sexuality, our talents, and our resources and patiently waits to see whether we will make good use of them.

God's punishments seem harsh, but they cannot be taken as a mature, well-rounded depiction of God's nature. Genesis is part of a gradual revelation of God to the community of faith. Even in these early stories, the narrator portrays a God who is concerned with justice, unlike the capricious deities of Israel's neighbors. For example, the narrator shows God fitting the punishment to the crime. For tempting the woman to eat forbidden fruit, the snake is condemned to eat dust; for committing a sin by eating, the man is punished by difficulty in obtaining food (3:14, 17–19). The ground that drank Abel's blood will no longer yield crops for his murderer (4:11–12). In the story of the flood, which we are about to read, the narrator will show the correspondence between people's wrongdoing and God's punishment by using the same word for both: the same Hebrew word lies behind "the earth was *corrupt* in God's sight" (6:11, italics mine) and "I am going to *destroy* them" (6:13, italics mine).

The poetic justice in these accounts indicates the functioning of a natural order. In the narrator's view, God created the world with a moral order, and violations of that order bring painful consequences. Sin cannot bring lasting happiness because it runs counter to the design of creation. While, in one sense, the punishments for sin in the Genesis accounts are personal judgments by God, they are, in another sense, the built-in results of tampering with the order that he has created.

God is forbearing in his dealings with humans even as he imposes penalties for sin. After sentencing Adam and Eve, God gives them durable clothing to replace the amateurish fig-leaf loincloths they hurriedly stitched together (3:7, 21). As he condemns Cain to a life of wandering, God puts his protection on him (4:15).

The narrator tells us that Seth has a son named Enosh (4:26). Both the name *Adam* and the name *Enosh* mean "human," but they have different connotations. *Adam* echoes the word for ground—the ground from which he is taken, which he is assigned to cultivate, and to which he will return (2:7, 15; 3:17, 19). *Enosh* is related to a word meaning "weak" or "frail." Nahum M. Sarna sees a connection between the birth of Enosh and the fact that "at that time people began to invoke the name of the LORD" (4:26): "It is the consciousness of human frailty, symbolized by the name Enosh, that heightens man's awareness of utter dependence upon God, a situation that intuitively evokes prayer." The "name of the LORD" is Yahweh, the personal name of God in the Hebrew Bible. Notably it is a woman, Eve, who first utters this personal name of God (4:1), but in a declaration rather than, as by Enosh (4:26), in prayer.

The notice that "at that time people began to invoke the name of the LORD" is interesting in another way. In the biblical story, God does not reveal his personal name until later, when he speaks to Moses from the burning bush (Exodus 3:15). But the Genesis narrator shows his awareness that even before God began to unfold his plan of salvation through the people of Israel, he made himself present to men and women—as God does to people today, whether or not they know about his supreme revelation of himself in his Son, Jesus Christ. As St. Paul indicated to an audience in Athens, God is not far from any of us but calls all men and women, in every place and religion, to seek and find him (Acts 17:22–31).

# GOD STARTS OVER

## Questions to Begin

*15 minutes*
*Use a question or two to get warmed up for the reading.*

**1** How did you learn to swim? If you never learned to swim, what held you back?

**2** Describe a situation in which you witnessed one person doing right despite the misguided attitudes or behavior of other people. What did you learn from this situation?

**Opening the Bible**

*5 minutes*
*Read the passage aloud. Let individuals take turns reading*
*paragraphs. (If participants have not already read "What's*
*Happened," read that aloud also. Otherwise skip it.)*

## What's Happened

Genesis continues with a genealogy tracing ten generations from
Adam (5:6–32), followed by fragmentary and very mysterious
references to divine beings and giants (6:1–4). After this, the
narrator takes up a much more familiar story: Noah and the flood.

## The Reading: Genesis 6:5–9:11

### A Disappointed Creator

5 The LORD saw that the wickedness of humankind was great in the
earth, and that every inclination of the thoughts of their hearts was
only evil continually. 6 And the LORD was sorry that he had made
humankind on the earth, and it grieved him to his heart. 7 So the
LORD said, "I will blot out from the earth the human beings I have
created—people together with animals and creeping things and birds
of the air, for I am sorry that I have made them." 8 But Noah found
favor in the sight of the LORD. . . .

13 And God said to Noah, "I have determined to make an
end of all flesh, for the earth is filled with violence because of them;
now I am going to destroy them along with the earth. 14 Make
yourself an ark of cypress wood; make rooms in the ark, and cover
it inside and out with pitch. . . . 17 For my part, I am going to bring
a flood of waters on the earth, to destroy from under heaven all flesh
in which is the breath of life; everything that is on the earth shall die.
18 But I will establish my covenant with you; and you shall come into
the ark, you, your sons, your wife, and your sons' wives with you.
19 And of every living thing, of all flesh, you shall bring two of every
kind into the ark, to keep them alive with you; they shall be male and
female. . . ." 22 Noah did this; he did all that God commanded him.

7:1 Then the LORD said to Noah, "Go into the ark, you and
all your household, for I have seen that you alone are righteous
before me in this generation." . . . 11 On that day all the fountains
of the great deep burst forth, and the windows of the heavens were
opened. . . . 17 The flood continued forty days on the earth; and
the waters increased, and bore up the ark, and it rose high above

the earth. . . . ¹⁹ The waters swelled so mightily on the earth that all
the high mountains under the whole heaven were covered. . . . ²¹ And
all flesh died that moved on the earth, birds, domestic animals, wild
animals, all swarming creatures that swarm on the earth, and all
human beings. . . .

8:1 But God remembered Noah and all the wild animals and
all the domestic animals that were with him in the ark. And God
made a wind blow over the earth . . . ² the rain from the heavens was
restrained, ³ and the waters gradually receded from the earth. . . .
¹⁸ So Noah went out with his sons and his wife and his sons' wives. . . .

## A Fresh Start

²⁰ Then Noah built an altar to the LORD, and took of every clean
animal and of every clean bird, and offered burnt offerings on the
altar. ²¹ And when the LORD smelled the pleasing odor, the LORD
said in his heart, "I will never again curse the ground because of
humankind, for the inclination of the human heart is evil from youth;
nor will I ever again destroy every living creature as I have done. . . ."

9:1 God blessed Noah and his sons, and said to them, "Be
fruitful and multiply, and fill the earth. ² The fear and dread of you
shall rest on every animal of the earth, and on every bird of the air,
on everything that creeps on the ground, and on all the fish of the sea;
into your hand they are delivered. ³ Every moving thing that lives
shall be food for you; and just as I gave you the green plants, I give
you everything. ⁴ Only, you shall not eat flesh with its life, that is, its
blood. ⁵ For your own lifeblood I will surely require a reckoning:
from every animal I will require it and from human beings, each one
for the blood of another, I will require a reckoning for human life.

⁶ Whoever sheds the blood of a human,
> by a human shall that person's blood be shed;
for in his own image
> God made humankind. . . .

⁹ As for me, I am establishing my covenant with you and your
descendants after you, ¹⁰ and with every living creature that is with
you, the birds, the domestic animals, and every animal of the earth
with you, as many as came out of the ark. ¹¹ I establish my covenant
with you, that never again shall all flesh be cut off by the waters of a
flood, and never again shall there be a flood to destroy the earth."

*10 minutes*
*Choose questions according to your interest and time.*

**1** How would you describe God's reaction to human wickedness in 6:5–7?

**2** Compare 6:5 and 8:21. How much did the flood change people? Why? What kind of change in people is needed?

**3** Compare 1:28–29 and 9:1–3. What are the differences and similarities between the commission that God gave at creation and the commission he gives at this second creation?

**4** In what ways do God's instructions in 9:1–6 show God making an accommodation to the condition of human beings recognized in 8:21?

## A Guide to the Reading

*If participants have not read this section already, read it aloud. Otherwise go on to "Questions for Application."*

The flood story is disturbing. Except for a handful of people, God wipes out the human race. Boys playing, grandmothers baking bread, farmers plowing their fields—all are washed away without so much as a "Heads up!" Could *all* have been so wicked (6:5, 11–13) as to deserve drowning? We can relieve ourselves of this and other insoluble questions (why didn't God send a prophet to warn people about the possibility of a flood?) by recalling that none of these early chapters of Genesis presents literal accounts. The flood story, like many other stories in these first chapters of Genesis, is not history (see the introduction, page 6). Like Eve's conversation with the snake, it is closer to a parable than to a newspaper report. Whatever judgment God actually brought on the human race in the long ages of prehistory, the specific events are hidden from us now. We can regard the Genesis account of the flood as teaching truths without believing that God actually destroyed everyone with a flood, just as we can regard Genesis 1 as teaching truths without holding that God's creative activity lasted six days.

The flood is such a drastic punishment for sin, it seems that God must have been angry, right? But the account nowhere speaks of God's wrath. It says he is "grieved"; it even tells us God is "sorry that he had made humankind" (6:6)—a bold way of expressing how thoroughly sickened God is at the sight of criminal violence and oppression (6:11, 13). Walter Brueggemann remarks that the account portrays God as an anguished parent rather than a wrathful tyrant. Think of a mother who sorrowfully reports her adult son's whereabouts to the police after he commits a crime.

The story may at first seem to focus on destruction, yet the doom of earth's inhabitants unfolds off camera without description (7:21–23). In the foreground of the picture is Noah and his family floating safely away, warned and carefully instructed by God. The accent is on salvation.

It is God, not skillful shipbuilding or plucky sailing, who saves Noah. The ark is an unwieldy houseboat—a rectangular box some 450 feet long, 75 feet wide, and 45 feet high (6:15). God shuts Noah in (7:16), and Noah cannot even see out, let alone steer (8:6–13). He is completely in God's hands.

In essence, the flood is a re-creation story. God undoes the first creation. He allows the waters of the ocean above the sky to pour down onto the earth and the waters under the earth to gush upward (7:11). The world returns to a condition of watery chaos (compare 1:2). Then God makes the human race anew. This time he does not form the human race from scratch, as in chapter 2, but he uses Noah and his family, like a baker of sourdough bread using some of the old starter for the new batch. The outcome is not the obliteration of the human race but a new arrangement between God and human beings, who are still made in his image (8:20–9:17).

The flood story may be read as an answer to the question "Why doesn't God put an end to the world when human beings' inhumanity toward each other descends to intolerable depths?" Surely this question has troubled many people in the course of history as they were driven onto slave ships or herded into gas chambers. To answer the question, the biblical story explores a test case: Suppose society became *utterly* corrupt. What would God do? The story suggests that, at least from the human point of view, God would show a certain ambivalence. He would bring judgment, yet he would wish human life to continue. God's rescue of Noah shows that despite human wrongdoing, God's impulse to save is stronger than his impulse to judge. Part of the answer, then, to why God allows the world to roll along despite human crimes is that he is constantly looking for ways to make a new start with his wayward human creatures.

God makes his policy of patience toward human beings explicit in the resolution of the story (8:21–22; 9:11–17). In 8:21 God shows the universal love that Jesus remarked on: God "makes his sun rise on the evil and on the good, and sends rain on the righteous and on the unrighteous"—a policy of forbearance that Jesus calls us to imitate (Matthew 5:44–45).

## Questions for Application

*40 minutes*
*Choose questions according to your interest and time.*

1   When has loss or failure led you to discover something about yourself that needed to change? What has been the long-term effect of this discovery?

2   When have you had the opportunity to make a fresh start? Did your old weaknesses and sins come along with you into the new situation? Did you experience new grace from God?

**3** How could you put into practice what Jesus recommends in Matthew 5:43–48?

**4** Through your family life, work, voluntary help, or political activity, how do you contribute to making the world a more just place? What one thing might you do differently?

**"When we share what the Bible means to us, we help others to articulate their own insights and their own faith."**

David Smith, *Guidebook for Bible Study*

## Approach to Prayer

*15 minutes*
*Use this approach — or create your own!*

---

✦ Have someone read Matthew
5:43–48 aloud. Give everyone
a few minutes for silent reflection. The Holy Spirit may
bring to mind someone to
forgive or a particular situation
where mercy is needed. Allow
for short, spontaneous prayers
if participants wish to offer any.
Close with an Our Father.

**Saints in the Making**

*An Ark for Today*

*This section is a supplement for individual reading.*

In 1964 a Canadian named Jean Vanier invited two men with mental and physical disabilities, Raphael and Philippe, to live with him. With Vanier providing the necessary care, the men kept house together, did a little gardening, cooked their meals, went to church, and prayed the rosary.

Vanier wrote afterward, "The idea of living happily together, of celebrating and laughing a lot, came quickly and spontaneously." Vanier's attitude shifted from simply *doing* things for the men to *listening* to them. "When the idea of the poor educating us came, I don't know exactly," Vanier wrote. "The words of St. Vincent de Paul, 'The poor are our masters,' were always there, but when they became a reality I'm uncertain.

"During those first months," Vanier recalled, "I was beginning to discover the immense amount of pain hidden in the hearts of Raphael and Philippe. At the same time I was beginning to discover some of the beauty and gentleness of their hearts, their capacity for communion and tenderness. I was beginning to sense how living with them could transform me."

Women in Trosly-Breuil, the French town where the men were living, brought gifts of food. A religious sister volunteered to cook meals. Vanier welcomed a third man with disabilities. A former art student, Jacqueline d'Halluin, began to come regularly to share in the work of the little household.

Vanier asked d'Halluin to write a prayer and help him choose a name for the budding community. The prayer she wrote addressed our Lady: "Mary, give us hearts that are attentive, humble, and gentle, so that we may welcome with tenderness and compassion all the poor you send us." D'Halluin suggested about a hundred names, drawn from the Bible. As soon as she mentioned the ark, Vanier knew that she had found the right name. "But it was only later on that I realized all the symbolism behind this biblical name," Vanier recalled.

Since 1964 the community of adults with disabilities and those who share their lives has grown and spread to many countries around the world. It is generally identified by the French form of its name: L'Arche (The Ark).

# *Between* Discussions

We can easily imagine that Noah and his family had a lot to keep them busy when they emerged from the ark— letting the animals go, unloading their belongings, setting up housekeeping in the mud. The narrator passes over such practical matters, however, and describes an action of a different sort. Noah built an altar, slaughtered animals, and burned them on the altar for God (8:20). This was the first act of humankind in the renewed, postflood creation.

You may recall that this is not the first mention of sacrifice in these Genesis stories of beginnings. Earlier Cain and Abel made offerings to God from flock and field (4:3–4).

Cain and Abel made their offerings in the course of the seasonal pattern of their lives, as crops matured and flocks reproduced and grew. Noah's offering was ad hoc, marking a unique event: the salvation of his family. But both types of sacrifice served the purpose of acknowledging that God is the source of life. The regular offerings of vegetables and fruit, sheep and cattle expressed the awareness that the vitality and fertility of plants and animals come from God. Noah's onetime offering on the damp hilltop was his way of acknowledging that he and his family owed their lives to God's action for them in the events of the flood.

These sacrifices connect with an important theme in Genesis—our being created in the image and likeness of God (1:26–27). The full meaning of our resemblance to God can never be fully grasped, because the God we resemble can never be fully grasped. But two aspects of our resemblance to him are in the foreground of the Genesis narrative.

First, in the ancient Near East, kings were considered images of God. For humans to be made in the image of God, then, means that we are placed here as royalty. We are commissioned to rule the earth on God's behalf. The earth will fulfill God's purposes as we rule it under his direction.

Second, our being in the image of God means that there is a match, a fit, between God and us that makes us capable of having a personal relationship with him. This makes us different from all the other creatures of the earth. We alone can recognize that the universe belongs to God and thank and praise him for his blessings.

The first aspect of our being made in God's image has us acting on behalf of God *toward creation,* caring for the earth according to his purposes. The second aspect has us acting on behalf of creation *toward God,* offering him thanks on behalf of the unreasoning, speechless creation. As one theologian has put it, we human beings are a kind of linchpin that God has put between himself and the rest of his creation.

The Genesis stories show that the first human beings carried out their role imperfectly, as have all of us since then. God continues to want the human race to play its assigned role, so he sent his Son to become one of us to play our part perfectly. As a human being like us, Jesus led a life of perfect love for other people, of perfect use of this world for God's purposes. Then he died as an offering of obedience to God, acknowledging that God is the giver of life, trusting that God would raise him up again. Thus Jesus fulfilled God's desire to have a perfect human representative *to his creation* and a perfect human offering of praise and thanksgiving *to God.* Jesus fulfilled both the earthward and the Godward roles for which God created us.

Now, as we are united with Jesus, God restores our ability to rule the earth according to his purposes and to live our lives in praise and thanks to him. It was in his death on the cross that Jesus showed both God's love to the world and his own love for the Father. Jesus' death was a great act of sacrifice. In the Eucharist, we share in Jesus' sacrifice. He draws us into his perfect offering of himself to his Father; united with Jesus we offer God thanks and praise for all he has made. At the same time, he nourishes us with his body and blood, enabling us to go forth and communicate God's peace and love to the world. In the Eucharist, the sacrifice that surpasses all the sacrifices of Genesis, God restores our ability to live out the earthward and Godward roles for which he has created us.

# The End of the Beginning

## Questions to Begin

*15 minutes*
*Use a question or two to get warmed up for the reading.*

**1** When have you felt frustrated by a language barrier?

**2** Besides language differences, what other barriers impede communication between people?

*5 minutes*
*Read the passage aloud. Let individuals take turns reading*
*paragraphs. (If participants have not already read "What's*
*Happened," read that aloud also. Otherwise skip it.)*

## What's Happened

The accounts of Adam and Eve and Cain and Abel deal with paradoxical facts of life. We humans desire to live forever, yet we die. Through work we fulfill God's purposes, yet work is hard and wearying. Childbirth—in which we are privileged to be cocreators with God—is accompanied by pain. Technology—by which we fulfill our assignment to rule the world—often has negative consequences. Why? The Genesis accounts point to a single answer. It was not the creator who introduced these regrettable contradictions into the human condition. Somehow—the Genesis accounts declare it without explaining it—we humans have undermined our own happiness by violating our God-given purposes and limitations.

After tracing some genealogies (chapter 10) the narrator now examines one further question about the human condition. Why do human beings, who have such marvelous God-given intelligence and belong basically to one family, often fail to understand each other? By this point in our reading, the answer should come as no surprise.

## The Reading: Genesis 11:1–12:5

### The Clash of Wills with God Continues

1 Now the whole earth had one language and the same words. 2 And as they migrated from the east, they came upon a plain in the land of Shinar and settled there. 3 And they said to one another, "Come, let us make bricks, and burn them thoroughly." And they had brick for stone, and bitumen for mortar. 4 Then they said, "Come, let us build ourselves a city, and a tower with its top in the heavens, and let us make a name for ourselves; otherwise we shall be scattered abroad upon the face of the whole earth." 5 The LORD came down to see the city and the tower, which mortals had built. 6 And the LORD said, "Look, they are one people, and they have all one language; and this is only the beginning of what they will do; nothing that they propose

to do will now be impossible for them. 7 Come, let us go down, and confuse their language there, so that they will not understand one another's speech." 8 So the LORD scattered them abroad from there over the face of all the earth, and they left off building the city. 9 Therefore it was called Babel, because there the LORD confused the language of all the earth; and from there the LORD scattered them abroad over the face of all the earth. . . .

## Abraham and Sarah Respond to God

27 Now these are the descendants of Terah. Terah was the father of Abram, Nahor, and Haran; and Haran was the father of Lot. 28 Haran died before his father Terah in the land of his birth, in Ur of the Chaldeans. 29 Abram and Nahor took wives; the name of Abram's wife was Sarai, and the name of Nahor's wife was Milcah. She was the daughter of Haran the father of Milcah and Iscah. 30 Now Sarai was barren; she had no child.

31 Terah took his son Abram and his grandson Lot son of Haran, and his daughter-in-law Sarai, his son Abram's wife, and they went out together from Ur of the Chaldeans to go into the land of Canaan; but when they came to Haran, they settled there. 32 The days of Terah were two hundred five years; and Terah died in Haran. 12:1 Now the LORD said to Abram, "Go from your country and your kindred and your father's house to the land that I will show you. 2 I will make of you a great nation, and I will bless you, and make your name great, so that you will be a blessing. 3 I will bless those who bless you, and the one who curses you I will curse; and in you all the families of the earth shall be blessed."

4 So Abram went, as the LORD had told him; and Lot went with him. Abram was seventy-five years old when he departed from Haran. 5 Abram took his wife Sarai and his brother's son Lot, and all the possessions that they had gathered, and the persons whom they had acquired in Haran; and they set forth to go to the land of Canaan.

*10 minutes*
*Choose questions according to your interest and time.*

**1**  What do the people wish to avoid (11:4)? How does their preference compare with God's commission to them (1:28; 9:1)? How does Abraham's response to God (12:1–5) compare with that of the people in 11:2–4?

**2**  God's assessment of the people in 11:6 ("Nothing that they propose to do will now be impossible for them") is similar in the Hebrew to the way Job describes what God does ("No purpose of yours can be thwarted"—Job 42:2). What does this similarity suggest about the root problem of the people at Shinar? How does this problem with the people at Shinar compare to the problem God faced with Adam and Eve (3:4, 22)? In what ways are the Eden and Babel stories similar?

## A Guide to the Reading

*If participants have not read this section already, read it aloud. Otherwise go on to "Questions for Application."*

God directed the first human beings to fill the earth (1:28; 9:1). But this does not suit the people at Shinar, who prefer to stay together and build a monument to their own greatness (11:4).

Both the couple in Eden and the people in Shinar choose independence rather than obedience and trust in God; they strive to exercise godlike control over their lives. The tower of Babel confirms the continuation of the sad state of affairs that God observed after the flood: "The inclination of the human heart is evil from youth" (8:21).

The story reflects the architecture and religion of Mesopotamia (present-day Iraq). The setting might have sounded as exotic to the story's original readers as it does to us. Notice that the narrator finds it necessary to explain why the people planned to use bricks and asphalt: "they had brick for stone, and bitumen for mortar" (11:3). Israelite readers were not acquainted with brick construction. In Israel there was plenty of stone and little water, so people did not generally build with bricks. Bricks were, however, the main building material in Mesopotamia, which had less stone but abundant mud. The Israelites, who lived in a hilly land, were probably also unfamiliar with the idea of building impressive towers for religious purposes. In Mesopotamia, however, where the land was relatively flat, people constructed artificial mountains—towers—to serve as high places where humans might make contact with the gods.

Just as in Eden, at Shinar humans "were no longer satisfied with the limited state of their existence, but wanted to force their way into the realm of the gods or God," Claus Westermann writes. The people's attempt to be godlike is a pathetic failure. As Nahum M. Sarna points out, the people proudly erect an impressive tower with its top in the sky (11:4), yet its height is insignificant to God, who has to go "down" to examine it (11:5). As always, the refusal to obey God ends in disaster (11:7–9). The story makes the point that if we reject the God who brings order out of chaos, our relationships with one another will become chaotic.

Various details reinforce this message. For example, the

Hebrew word for bricks (11:3) is echoed in the word for confuse (11:7). This subtly suggests that grasping for godlike status ensures its doom. Evil is a boomerang.

Unlike the preceding stories, the account of the people who built the tower of Babel ends without consolation. God made clothes for the first couple; he put a mark of protection on the first murderer; he established a covenant with the survivors of the flood. But the Babel story breaks off without any amelioration of judgment. We are left to wonder whether God has any further plans for his wayward human creatures. Has a basically hopeless dynamic now been established for human history? Will God's masterpieces—human beings—simply continue to grieve him by overstepping their creaturely limits and playing god over their own lives? These marvelous creatures, who are still in God's image and still cocreators and coworkers with him, now live under the shadow of pain, toil, disharmony, and death. Does God plan to straighten out this sad situation?

With the appearance of Terah (11:27), we have arrived at a new era. The narrative leaves behind parable-like stories of origins and emerges onto the stage of history. Events now occur in historical places, such as Ur and Haran (in present-day Iraq and Turkey—11:31). The focus narrows down, from the ancestors of the entire human race to one particular family—the family of Terah's son Abram, ancestor of the people Israel. With the first eleven chapters fresh in our minds, we may well suspect that God's dealings with this one family will have implications for the whole world.

Abraham believes God's rather improbable promises and responds to God's exceptionally demanding summons (12:1–4; it is customary to refer to Abram and Sarai by the adjusted names God later gives them: Abraham and Sarah—17:5, 15). With his wife, Abraham turns away from the distrust and disobedience toward God that have brought the human race into difficulties. Thus he sets the standard for human responses to the plan that God is going to unfold. For God does indeed have a plan to straighten out the mess that human sin has caused—a plan that will culminate in Jesus of Nazareth's perfect trust in and obedience to God.

## Questions for Application

*40 minutes*
*Choose questions according to your interest and time.*

**1** Think of someone with whom you have difficulty communicating. How have you contributed to a barrier to honest communication? What might you do to overcome the barrier?

**2** In 11:7, God says literally, "Come, let us go down, and confuse their language there, so that they will not *hear* one another's speech." How much of the misunderstandings between people stem from not listening? How carefully do you listen to other people? What could you do to increase the degree to which you truly hear what other people are saying?

**3** When, in your relationships with other people, have you experienced greater harmony as the result of following God's commandments?

**4** Where might God be calling you to make a departure from the familiar into the unfamiliar? What should your response be?

**"The word of God is frozen in dead letters in a book. It must be thawed out by the warm breath of love and prayer, to become a living stream that flows into our minds and souls."**

James Rauner, *The Young Church in Action*

## Approach to Prayer

*15 minutes*
*Use this approach — or create your own!*

---

✦ The gift of the Holy Spirit, given to Jesus' followers after his return to the Father, can reverse the confusion and division of Babel. Pray for the Spirit to work in your own relationships:

Have someone read aloud the account of Pentecost, which describes the Spirit beginning to undo the language barrier thrown up as a consequence of human pride at Babel (Acts 2:1–11).

Let participants mention relationships in which there are barriers of bitterness or misunderstanding. After each one, let the group pray, "Come, Holy Spirit, bring healing, hearing, and understanding."

End with an Our Father.

**Saints in the Making**

*Far from Home?*

*This section is a supplement for individual reading.*

For years my friend Rosaleen taught in an elementary school in Michigan. But some time ago, politics in the school system began to get her down. She also developed a back problem that occasionally kept her out of the classroom for weeks at a time. She had many friends and, in many ways, a comfortable life, but she began to sense the need for a change.

A religious sister asked Rosaleen whether she had ever considered missionary work. This suggestion struck a chord. But where? Doing what?

Rosaleen knew some people who had begun to visit Lithuania to provide support to the Catholic Church there. Through them, the possibility developed of Rosaleen's going to live for a year in Lithuania. She was interested, but unsure. So many things would need to fall into place. When her back problem led to her receiving an early retirement, the way seemed to open. Rosaleen rented out her condo and took a seven-thousand-mile step in faith. She flew off to Lithuania to teach English at a seminary.

Shortly after arriving, Rosaleen reported back to her friends in Michigan. "I feel I have fallen in love with these people." The lay community that extended hospitality to her arranged a welcoming dinner, and Rosaleen felt "an immediate sense of family." "I knew right away that these are my brothers and sisters in Christ," she said. "More than that, I experienced the awe-inspiring presence of Jesus in this poor place.

"I hesitate to describe the living conditions," she said. "What we would consider the greatest of hardships is a way of life here. Everything appears run down; buildings are falling apart; the flats are bleak. Yet how can I describe the life that I have found here? Amid incredibly difficult conditions, grace abounds. I feel the presence of Jesus so near and so real. I am so very happy here and am wondering already how I will ever leave this place and these people."

That was five years ago. Rosaleen is still living and working with Christians in Lithuania. In one sense, she is far from home. But she has found a new home. Like Abraham and Sarah, she heard a call to go out. In responding to the call, she has found more than she could have expected.

# *After* Words

I t would be hard to exaggerate the importance of Abraham. The term *pivotal figure* might have been created to describe him. The story of Abraham and Sarah marks a transition from one period to another. When Abraham appears in Genesis 12, the period of the beginning of the human race comes to an end; God's action in historical times gets under way. Unlike Adam, Eve, Cain, Abel, and Noah, Abraham is not an archetypal figure, not an ancestor of the human race. He is simply one of the thousands of sheep and cattle breeders who lived in eastern Syria roughly four thousand years ago. Abraham and Sarah are ordinary people, called by God to play a part in his grand plan for the human race. From them to us stretches an uninterrupted line of divine activity, running through the history of Israel, culminating in Jesus of Nazareth, and continuing through the centuries in the life of the Church.

Abraham was the ancestor of the Israelites. It was one of his grandsons, Jacob, also called Israel, who gave his name to the people. Members of Israel referred to themselves as descendants of Abraham—an expression of identity heard in the Gospels (John 8:33).

In the history of Israel, however, another figure loomed larger: Moses. He led the people of Israel through their formative events: the escape from Egypt and the covenant with God at Sinai. Moses was considered the author of the first five books of the Bible, which record the basic instruction for Israel's life with God. Since the people's relationship with God centered on a reverent application of this instruction to their lives, Moses occupied—and still occupies—a position at the center of Israel's experience.

For Christians, Jesus displaced Moses from this central role. Jesus respected the Mosaic law but taught that it did not perfectly reflect God's intentions for human life (Matthew 5:17–48). In fulfillment of the law, Jesus offered himself—the model of complete trust in and obedience to God and of perfect love for human beings. By his death and resurrection, and the gift of the Spirit, Jesus undertook the transformation of human hearts so that we might have a relationship with God even deeper than that shaped by the Mosaic instruction (Hebrews 10:12–17).

In the view of St. Paul, Jesus brought to completion the period of God's plan that began with Moses. Because God's activity reached its climax in Jesus, Paul says, God's people should orient their lives not by faithfulness to the Mosaic law, whose importance has been overshadowed by Jesus, but by imitation of Abraham, whose example will always remain valid (Galatians 3). With Moses displaced, Jesus' followers could look back directly to Abraham, with whom God's activity had begun.

The account of Abraham and Sarah that we read in Week 6, short as it is, contains the essence of their story. They listened to God, they believed what God promised them, and they did what God told them to do. These are the reasons the New Testament writers point to Abraham as the model for and spiritual ancestor of God's people (Galatians 3:6; James 2:21–24).

Genesis 12:1, as Nahum M. Sarna observes, underlines the enormity of God's demands on Abraham and Sarah by arranging them in ascending order of severity: they were to give up "country, extended family, nuclear family." Even more difficult, they were challenged to believe the virtually impossible. How could they, who had had no children during the long years of their marriage, have offspring through whom a great people would arise? To act on this promise was to build their lives on trust that God is the Lord and giver of life (see Hebrews 11:8–12, 17–19). Thus Abraham and Sarah exemplify what is at the heart of all human response to God.

Repeatedly, in following Jesus, we must leave behind beloved people and things in order to set out in directions where we sense God's invitation. Each time, we face the question of whether we trust that God is able to create new life, whether he has a plan for our lives, whether he will be faithful to us. These were the questions that Abraham and Sarah faced and answered. We can take this couple as our model.

Through Abraham's and Sarah's trust and obedience, God set in motion a plan for all humankind. Who knows what part of that plan God might accomplish through our willingness to hear an unexpected call from him, through our obedience and trust?

## A Book for Today

The Bible has been described as the user's manual for the universe. The statement is half right. The Bible is not a handbook containing how-to answers to all our questions. But it is the creator's basic written message to us concerning his purposes for our lives and his relationship with us.

Reading and rereading the opening chapters of Genesis in the course of writing this booklet, I have been impressed by their relevance to issues we face today. Of course, the Genesis accounts, written two and a half millennia ago, do not deal directly with specific modern issues. But they convey a great deal about God's intentions and his view of us—an invaluable background for our thinking. Here are observations on three areas where Genesis touches on modern concerns.

**The environment.** Awareness of humans' damage to the environment has grown in recent decades, and some people have accused the Bible of contributing to the problem. Critics especially target Genesis 1. They claim that by insisting that there is only one God, who utterly transcends the universe, the Bible has exposed nature to human exploitation: once the deities of rain and soil and fertility were stripped away, nature no longer seemed sacred, only useful. Moreover, critics allege, the command to humanity to "subdue" and "have dominion over" the earth (1:28) has provided a rationale for disregarding the damage we inflict on the environment.

There may be some truth to allegations that people have sometimes appealed to the Bible to defend exploitation of the environment. If so, however, the problem lies in false interpretation of the Bible rather than in the Bible itself.

When the nature deities are driven from people's minds by faith in the one God, the earth is not exposed to abuse, for it belongs to God. God puts the man in the garden to "keep," or protect, it (2:15), not to destroy it. The man is a caretaker, responsible to the owner for maintaining the property in good condition.

God's command to us to rule the earth is not a license to treat the natural world with disdain. Father Bruce Vawter points out that while the Hebrew word translated "subdue" is a "verb of some vehemence," human subduing of the earth is not supposed to be a ruthless dominance. "It was to be, rather, a domination modeled on God's own," Father Vawter explains. The creation accounts show God ordering the universe and approving its purposefulness. We, as his representatives, are responsible for understanding and maintaining God's order and achieving his purposes for creation.

Nahum M. Sarna adds another reason the power given to humans in Genesis 1:28 does not include "the license to exploit nature banefully." While God established humans as kings over the earth, Sarna writes, "the model of kingship here presupposed is Israelite, according to which, the monarch does not possess unrestrained power and authority." Just as Israelite kings were supposed to shepherd the people, not oppress them, humanity is supposed to care for the earth, not rape it.

A careful reading of Genesis 1, then, leads us toward respect, rather than disdain, for the environment. One contemporary strategy, however, for fostering harmony between humans and the natural world runs counter to the viewpoint of Genesis. In a desire to emphasize our dependence on the environment and to protect other living things from abuse, some environmentalists seem to propose a kind of equality between humans and other life-forms. They speak of humans as simply one of earth's many species, with no more or less right to live than any of the others. The Genesis accounts, however, draw a sharp, distinguishing line between the human race and all other species.

The account of creation in Genesis 1 shows that God assigns a unique status to the human race. St. Gregory of Nyssa, a fourth-century theologian, remarks that up to verse 26, chapter 1 shows "the divine power, as one might say, 'improvising' creation, which comes into existence as soon as it is commanded. On the contrary, for the formation of humankind a deliberation precedes, and a plan is first established. It is only for the creation of humankind that the author of the universe advances with circumspection." Humans alone are created in the image and likeness of God, which gives us a unique relationship with God and an assignment to rule the earth (1:27–28).

The account in Genesis 2 reinforces the radical distinction between humanity and other species. God brings the animals before the man to be named, thus showing the man's authority over them. Among the animals, "there was not found a helper as his partner" (2:20). Claus Westermann remarks that the author of this verse wanted "to stress the difference between a human being and a beast."

**Sex.** Genesis says nothing directly about the various sexual issues we face in the modern world. But, again, it provides invaluable background for our thinking.

Consider, for example, the widespread acceptance of sex outside marriage, in light of these elements of the Genesis account:

✦ According to Genesis 2, the purpose of human sexuality lies in man and woman becoming so united as to be "one flesh" (2:24).

✦ The account suggests that the bond between the man and the woman provides the opportunity for them to know themselves as they otherwise could not. In naming the woman, the man refers to himself for the first time with the ordinary Hebrew word for adult male: "This one shall be called Woman, for out of Man this one was taken" (2:23). It seems that in coming to know the woman the man comes to know himself.

✦ The narrator says that the man knows his wife (4:1). This term for sexual intercourse is not a euphemism—a way of speaking about sex indirectly—but a term of great significance. The biblical writers apply this expression for sexual intercourse only to humans, never to animals. *Knowing* indicates the personal, more-than-biological dimension of human sexuality. The term testifies to the profoundly relational quality of human sex.

All these points are indications of the depth God intends for the human sexual relationship. In light of this divine purpose, doesn't every uncommitted, casual, or recreational use of sex seem like an impoverished distortion?

Another subject to which Genesis is relevant is the Catholic teaching about the link between sexual intercourse and reproduction. The Church teaches that, in God's purposes, intercourse and reproduction—the person-uniting and person-creating aspects of human sex—belong together. Artificial contraception represents one attempt to deliberately separate these two aspects of sex; artificial insemination represents another. The Church teaches us that neither attempt is moral.

Many Catholics do not accept this teaching, and for many years I was among them. But I began to see that underlying my objections to this teaching was an unexamined resistance. It simply seemed implausible to me that there could be *any* good reason to refrain from using available technologies to control what could be controlled in this area of life. I think I am typical in this regard. Living in a technological culture, we are used to maximizing our control over every aspect of life. It seems normal to us to use technology whenever it can help us achieve our purposes. Given this mind-set, it is almost impossible for us to be convinced by any arguments, no matter how substantial, that we should refrain from using technology to determine such an important area of our lives as sex and reproduction.

As I now read the Genesis accounts, I notice two considerations that raise questions about this almost automatic tendency to take technological control of our sexuality. First is the profound interest that God takes in human sexuality. Sex is, indeed, the first topic on which God speaks to human beings: "God blessed them, and God said to them, 'Be fruitful and multiply, and fill the earth'" (1:28). The blessing that God gives the first couple is a sharing in his own creative power. God's blessing is the capacity he gives us to fulfill his command to be fruitful, the fertility that he places within us (compare 1:22). In the process of having children we are cocreators with God, as Eve recognized when she greeted Cain's birth with words that may be translated, "I have created a man with the Lord" (4:1).

The second consideration is our fateful, self-deluded tendency to take control of our lives, as portrayed in Genesis 3. The issue symbolized by the prohibition against eating from the tree of the knowledge of good and evil is whether the man and the woman will acknowledge a creaturely limit to their freedom—a limit that they cannot fully understand but can keep only in a spirit of obedience to and trust in God.

This pair of considerations helps me as I reflect on the Church's teaching against artificially separating the person-uniting and person-creating dimensions of sex. Neither consideration speaks directly to the issues involved, but they lead me to examine the teaching in a different frame of mind from that of our technological culture. Genesis reminds me that in our sexuality we touch on something especially important to God. Our creator is profoundly present with us in this dimension of our lives. Should we not, then, be especially serious in searching out God's purposes for our sexuality? The drama in the garden invites us to recognize our inclination to violate creaturely limits and play god over our lives. Might this inclination be at work in our modern attitudes toward sex and reproduction?

**Human life.** Abortion and capital punishment are currently divisive issues concerning society's valuation and treatment of human life. In Genesis we find much that is significant for both issues.

Actually, the fundamental question about abortion is not religious but biological: is the fetus a human being? As Carol Crossed writes, "The onset of human life is not a religious dogma but a fact of science. The humanity of the unborn child is not found in the Bible or the tenets of Christianity or Buddhism, but rather in a college textbook on embryology." However, once we accept the scientific finding that the fetus is a distinct genetic entity, that is, a separate human life, Genesis helps us understand how we should treat this life.

Genesis tells us that God created the human race in his image and likeness. In the biblical tradition it has always been recognized that each individual shares in this divine likeness. Regarding 1:26–28, Nahum M. Sarna writes that the sages of Jewish tradition "observed that mankind was created as a single unit in order to indicate the idea that the destruction of a single life is tantamount to the destruction of the entire world and, conversely, the preservation of a single life is the preservation of the entire world."

God's anguished response to Abel's murder makes clear how seriously God regards the destruction of a single human life (4:10–11). And God's protection of Cain (4:13–15) shows how highly God continues to value the life even of one who has taken life. This point leads us to consider how the Genesis accounts might speak to the issue of capital punishment.

Although God protects Cain from vengeance, farther on in the narrative God gives instructions for the execution of murderers (9:5–6). This action might seem to reverse the more benign approach God took toward Cain. The underlying principle in both passages, however, is the same: human life is inviolable because it belongs to God. The directive to impose capital punishment in chapter 9 arises from a change in circumstances within the narrative. Capital punishment has become necessary to defend life because human beings have become so violent (6:11).

Capital punishment was practiced throughout the ancient Near East, as it has been in many societies throughout history. Capital punishment, slavery, warfare that placed civilian populations under the ban—these and other inhumane practices that marred the early stages of the Israelite tradition were reflections of the cultural environment the community was coming from, not the purposes of God toward which it was journeying. The revelation of God's mercy and love worked gradually within the community of faith as a leaven—as it continues to do today.

Regarding capital punishment, the element from Genesis that has enduring validity is the principle that humans are created in God's image, not the instruction to impose capital punishment. God's treatment of Cain demonstrates his preference for protecting the life even of someone who has killed. Today it is possible to protect human life without imposing capital punishment for murder. The call in contemporary Catholic teaching to end capital punishment in virtually all situations is in keeping with the biblical tradition, which emphasizes the value of each human life.

## Suggestions for Bible Discussion Groups

L ike a camping trip, a Bible discussion group works best if you agree on what you're undertaking together, why you're doing it, where you hope to get to, and how you intend to get there. Many groups use their first meeting to reach a consensus on such questions. Here is a checklist of issues, with a few bits of advice from people with experience in Bible discussions. (A planning discussion will go more smoothly if the leaders have thought through the following issues beforehand.)

**Agree on your purpose.** Are you getting together to gain wisdom and direction for your life? to finally get acquainted with the Bible? to support one another in following Christ? to encourage those who are exploring—or reexploring—the Church? for other reasons?

**Agree on attitudes.** For example: "We're all beginners here." "We're here to help each other understand and respond to God's Word." "We're not here to offer counseling or direction to each other." "We want to read Scripture prayerfully." What do *you* wish to emphasize? Make it explicit!

**Agree on ground rules.** Barbara J. Fleischer, in her useful book *Facilitating for Growth,* recommends that a group clearly state its approach to the following:

✦ Preparation. Do we agree to read the material before each meeting?

✦ Attendance. What kind of priority will we give to our meetings?

✦ Self-revelation. Are we willing to help the others in the group gradually get to know us—our weaknesses as well as our strengths, our needs as well as our gifts?

✦ Listening. Will we commit ourselves to listening to each other?

✦ Confidentiality. Will we keep everything that is shared with the group in the group?

✦ Encouragement and support. Will we give as well as receive?

✦ Participation. Will we work to allow everyone time and opportunity to make a contribution?

You could probably take a pen and draw a circle around *listening* and *confidentiality.* Those two points are especially important.

The following items could be added to Fleischer's list:

✦ Relationship with parish. Is our group part of the religious education program? independent but operating with the express approval of the pastor? not a parish-based group at all?

✦ New members. In the course of the six meetings, will new members be allowed?

### Agree on housekeeping.

✦ When will we meet?

✦ How often will we meet? Meeting weekly or every other week is best if you can manage it. William Riley remarks, "Meetings once a month are too distant from each other for the threads of the last session not to be lost" *(The Bible Study Group: An Owner's Manual).*

✦ How long will meetings run?

✦ Where will we meet?

✦ Is any setup needed? Christine Dodd writes that "the problem with meeting in a place like a church hall is that it can be very soul-destroying" given the cold, impersonal feel of many church facilities. If you have to meet in a church facility, Dodd recommends doing something to make the area homey *(Making Scripture Work).*

✦ Who will host the meetings? Leaders and hosts are not necessarily identical.

✦ Will we have refreshments? Who will provide them?

✦ What about child care? Most experienced leaders of Bible discussion groups discourage bringing infants or other children to adult Bible discussions.

**Agree on leadership.** You need someone to facilitate—to keep the discussion on track, to see that everyone has a chance to speak, to help the group stay on schedule. Rena Duff, editor of the newsletter *Sharing God's Word Today,* recommends having two or three people take turns leading the discussions.

It's okay if the leader is not an expert regarding the Bible. You have this booklet, and if questions come up that no one can answer, you can delegate a participant to do a little research between meetings. It's important for the leader to set an example of listening, to draw out the quieter members (and occasionally restrain the more vocal ones), to move the group on when it gets stuck, to remind the members of their agreements, and to summarize what the group is accomplishing.

Bible discussion is an opportunity to experience the fulfillment of Jesus' promise "Where two or three are gathered in my name, I am there among them" (Matthew 18:20). Put your discussion group in Jesus' hands. Pray for the guidance of the Spirit. And have a great time exploring God's Word together!

**Suggestions for Individuals**

You can use this booklet just as well for individual study as for group discussion. While discussing the Bible with other people can be a rich experience, there are advantages to individual reading. For example:

✦ You can focus on the points that interest you most.

✦ You can go at your own pace.

✦ You can be completely relaxed and unashamedly honest in your answers to all the questions, since you don't have to share them with anyone else!

My suggestions for using this booklet on your own are these:

✦ Don't skip "Questions to Begin." The questions can help you as an individual reader warm up to the topic of the reading.

✦ Take your time on "Questions for Careful Reading" and "Questions for Application." While a group will probably not have enough time to work on all the questions, you can allow yourself the time to consider all of them if you are using the booklet by yourself.

✦ If you are going through Genesis at your own pace, read the portions that are skipped in the weekly sessions. Your total understanding of Genesis 1–11 will be greatly increased by reading the chapters in their entirety.

✦ Since you control the pace, give yourself plenty of opportunities to reflect on the meaning of Genesis for you. Let your reading be an opportunity for the words of Genesis to become God's words to you.

## Bibles

The following editions of the Bible contain the full set of biblical books recognized by the Catholic Church, along with a great deal of useful explanatory material:

✦ The Catholic Study Bible (Oxford University Press), which uses the text of the New American Bible

✦ The Catholic Bible: Personal Study Edition (Oxford University Press), which also uses the text of the New American Bible

✦ The New Jerusalem Bible, the regular (not the standard or reader's) edition (Doubleday)

## Books

✦ Walter Brueggemann, *Genesis: A Bible Commentary for Preaching and Teaching* (Atlanta: John Knox Press, 1982).

✦ Nahum M. Sarna, *Genesis: The Traditional Hebrew Text with New JPS Translation* (Philadelphia: Jewish Publication Society, 1989).

✦ Bruce Vawter, *On Genesis: A New Reading* (Garden City, N.Y.: Doubleday, 1977).

✦ Gerhard von Rad, *Genesis: A Commentary,* The Old Testament Library (Philadelphia: Westminster Press, 1973).

✦ Claus Westermann, *Genesis 1–11,* Continental Commentary (Minneapolis: Fortress Press, 1994).

How has Scripture had an impact on your life? Was this booklet helpful to you in your study of the Bible? Please send comments, suggestions, and personal experiences to Kevin Perrotta c/o Trade Editorial Department, Loyola Press, 3441 N. Ashland Ave., Chicago, IL 60657.